MW01717306

New York State Comprehensive School Counseling Program:

High School Activity Book

ISBN 1-59113-614-8

Printed in the United States of America.

ACTIVITY BOOK TASK FORCE

Emily Phillips, Ph. D.
Assistant Professor, Counselor Education
State University of New York, College at Oneonta

Christi Smith
School Counselor
Vestal Central Schools
Vestal, New York

Lucinda Steele
School Counselor
Vestal Central Schools
Vestal, New York

Clerical and Editorial Assistance

Amber Haggerty
Graduate Student
State University of New York, College at Oneonta

Courtney Colliton
Graduate Student
State University of New York, College at Oneonta

Charlita Ryan
Secretary
State University of New York, College at Oneonta

NYS Comprehensive School Counseling Program Committee

Carol Dahir Ed.D., Counselor Education, New York Institute of Technology
David Ford, School Counselor, Queensbury High School
Deborah Hardy, School Counseling Department Chair, Irvington High/Middle School
Doug Morrissey, School Counselor, Canajoharie High School

Message from the Editor

This book is designed as a companion text to NYSSCA's New York State Comprehensive School Counseling Program Model (2003). This model is based on American School Counselors' Associations' National Standards for School Counseling Programs (1997) and attends to academic, vocational, and personal/social needs of children in New York State. There are three activity manuals: Elementary, Middle, and Secondary levels.

The following activities were designed to assist with operationalizing these standards. The majority of the lessons were revised from an earlier edition of these manuals. Most lessons are original. Original or cited as best we could as an adaptation from a published source. These lessons have been designed by practicing school counselors, a counselor educator with a school counseling background, and a few graduate students as part of course assignments in counselor education programs. We expect you to photocopy any you can use, and we provided multiple lessons for each objective in order to get you started. Each lesson is cross-referenced to the New York State Learning or ASCA standards. A chart in the back of the book can help you readily access lessons on a particular topic or covering a particular standard.

Without the dedication of the members of the Task Force, and of the other contributors, this book would not be a reality. The tireless efforts of NYSSCA presidents, the endless task of typing, the tremendous effort to code and format this set of manuals is unimaginable. Without the support of our department, students, graduates, secretaries, and practicing school counselors, this project could not have been undertaken. This set is the result of a grass roots effort to improve best practice in the field of school counseling. We hope we have provided a concrete and useful publication that serves as a guideline to operationalizing the national and state standards.

Enjoy this book. Use it as is, or for ideas to launch your own creativity. The best accolade that this project can receive is to see copies of it tattered, with pages falling out of it from overuse. Remember, this is our best effort to align these lessons with national and state standards. You may find that a number of these match a greater number of standards than we considered.

Emily Phillips, Ph.D., N.C.C.
Counselor Education
SUNY College at Oneonta

A Message From The President

The New York State School Counselor Association is honored to release this document and its companion activity manuals. The culmination of many months of work on the part of people from across the state, NYSSCA's activity manuals are the third and final installment in the Association's *New York State Comprehensive School Counseling Program*. Other components of this project include the *New York State Comprehensive School Counseling Program* text and the *New York State Comprehensive School Counseling Program Crosswalk* that links the National Standards for School Counseling Programs with the New York State Learning Standards.

Professional school counseling has undergone a significant transformation in the last several years. As the education reform movement has grown in American, school counseling has changed to meet society's new demands. The introduction of the American School Counselor Association's National Standards for School Counseling Programs in the 1990s followed by that association's *National Model for School Counseling Programs* (2003), brought us into the 21st Century as a standards-based, data driven profession accountable for student achievement. The three components of NYSSCA's *New York State Comprehensive School Counseling Program* do the same for school counseling in the Empire State's challenging educational environment.

I hope you will look upon the activities in these pages as a gift from your colleagues around the state. These professionals took the time to share their best practices with all of us for the benefit of students across the state. We all owe them a debt of gratitude. Thanks to their efforts, we've begun to build a library of resources we can all draw upon in our day-to-day work. NYSSCA thanks Dr. Emily Phillips, from SUNY Oneonta, and her colleagues. Without their work, these books would not exist. We also thank Deborah Hardy, of Irvington High School in Westchester County. A long-time leader in our field, Deb has overseen all parts of the *New York State Comprehensive School Counseling Program*. Without her guiding vision, this project would have never seen the light of day.

NYSSCA is the only organization in New York State dedicated to the development of professional school counseling for the benefit of students. As a chartered division of the American School Counselor Association, NYSSCA provides leadership, professional development and resources, like the one in your hand, to practicing school counselors, graduate students, counselor educators, and others interested in the profession. If you're interested in learning more about the Association or getting more involved, visit our website at www.NYSSCA.org. Your involvement can help shape the face of profession!

Douglas Morrissey
Canajoharie High School
NYSSCA President, 2004-2005

Table of Content

Preface

Standards will remain simply statements of what students should know and be able to do until they are brought to life. Once they are integrated across the comprehensive and developmental school counseling program, the standards take on meaningful importance. School counselors can now better ascertain how the results of focused efforts can contribute to every student's academic, career, and personal-social development and to school improvement. New York State school counselors, under the coordinated and editorial efforts of Emily Philips, Ph.D. have contributed their very best to show us ways of integrating the National Standards across grades K through 12 and connecting the school counseling program to the NYS Academic Learning standards.

Best Practices will:

- Provide replicable activities in a simple step-by-step process;
- Encourage school counselors to identify the ways that they impact the instructional program and contribute to student achievement;
- Promote school counselor leadership, advocacy, collaboration, use of data, and technology.
- Help administrators, teachers, and others understand how the work of school counselors contributes to school improvement and systemic change; and,
- Motivate school counselors to align their work with the ASCA National Standards and the NYSSCA l Model.

When New York State school counselors focus their efforts on the mission of school improvement, they widen educational opportunities for every student and can positively impact student achievement. New York State school counselors are leading the way.

Carol Dahir Ed.D.
Counselor Education
New York Institute of Technology

American School Counselors Associations
National Standards for School Counseling Programs

Competencies and Indicators

Academic Development

Standard A: ***Academic Standard A*****: Students will acquire the attitudes, knowledge, and skills that contribute to effective learning in school and across the life span.**

A: A1: Improve Academic Self Concept

A: A1 .1: Articulate feelings of competence and confidence as learners
A: A1 .2: Display a positive interest in learning
A: A1 .3: Take pride in work and achievement
A: A1 .4: Accept mistakes as essential to the learning process
A: A1 .5: Identify attitudes which lead to successful learning

A: A2: Acquire Skills for Improving Learning

A: A2 .1: Apply time management and task management skills
A: A2 .2: Demonstrate how effort and persistence positively affect learning
A: A2 .3: Use communication skills to know when and how to ask for help when needed
A: A2 .4: Apply knowledge and learning styles to positively influence school performance
A: A2 .5; Refine study and organizational skills

A: A3: Achieve School Success

A: A3 .1: Take responsibility for their actions
A: A3 .2: Demonstrate the ability to work independently, as well as the ability to work cooperatively with others
A: A3 .3: Develop a broad range of interests and abilities
A: A3 .4: Demonstrate dependability, productivity, and initiative
A: A3 .5: Share knowledge

Standard B: **Students will complete school with the academic preparation essential to choose from a wide range of substantial postsecondary options, including college.**

A: B1: Improve Learning

A: B1 .1: Demonstrate the motivation to achieve individual potential
A: B1 .2: Learn and apply critical thinking skills
A: B1 .3: Apply the study skills necessary for academic success at each level
A: B1 .4: Seek information and support from faculty, staff, family and peers
A: B1 .5: Organize and apply academic information from a variety of sources
A: B1 .6: Use knowledge of learning styles to positively influence school performance
A: B1 .7: Become a self – directed and independent learner

A: B2: Plan to Achieve Goal

A: B2 .1: Establish challenging academic goals to elementary, middle/junior high, and high school
A: B2 .2: Develop an initial four-year plan
A: B2 .3: Update and modify four-year plan
A: B2 .4: Use assessment results in educational planning
A: B2 .5: Develop and implement annual plan of study to maximize academic ability and achievement
A: B2 .6: Apply knowledge of aptitudes and interests to goal setting
A: B2 .7: Use problem solving and decision making skills to assess progress toward educational goals
A: B2 .8: Understand the relationship between classroom performance and success in school
A: B2 .9: Identify post-secondary options consistent with interests, achievement, aptitude, and abilities

Standard C: **Students will understand the relationship of academics to the world of work, and to life at home and in the community**

A: C1: Relate School to life Experiences

A: C1 .1: Demonstrate the ability to balance school, studies, extracurricular activities, leisure time, and family life
A: C1 .2: Seek co – curricular and community experiences to enhance the school experience
A: C1 .3: Understand the relationship between learning and work

A: C1 .4: Demonstrate an understanding of the value of lifelong learning as essential to seeking, obtaining, and maintaining life goals
A: C1 .5: Understand that school success is the preparation to make the transition from student to community member
A: C1 .6: Understand how school success and academic achievement enhance future career and vocational opportunities

Career Development

***Standard A*: Students will acquire the skills to investigate the world of work in relation to knowledge of self and to make informed career decisions**

C: A1: Develop Career Awareness

C: A1 .1: Develop skills to locate, evaluate, and interpret career information
C: A1 .2: Learn about the variety of traditional and non – traditional occupations
C: A1 .3: Develop an awareness of personal abilities, skills, interests, and motivations
C: A1 .4: Learn how to interact and work cooperatively in teams
C: A1 .5: Learn to make decisions
C: A1 .6: Learn how to set goals
C: A1 .7: Understand the importance of planning
C: A1 .8: Pursue and develop competency in areas of interest
C: A1 .9: Develop hobbies and vocational interests
C: A1 .10: Balance between work and leisure time

C: A 2: Develop Employment Readiness

C: A2 .1: Acquire employability skills such as working on a team, problem solving and organizational skills
C: A2 .2: Apply job readiness skills to seek employment opportunities
C: A2 .3: Demonstrate knowledge about the changing workplace
C: A2 .4: Learn about the rights and responsibilities of employers and employees
C: A2 .5: Learn to respect individual uniqueness in the workplace
C: A2 .6: Learn how to write a resume
C: A2 .7: Develop a positive attitude toward work and learning
C: A2 .8: Understand the importance of responsibility, dependability, punctuality, integrity, and effort in the workplace
C: A2 .9: Utilize time and task management skills

Standard B: **Students will employ strategies to achieve future career goals with success and satisfaction.**

C: B1: Acquire Career Information

C: B1 .1: Apply decision making skills to career planning, course selection, and career transition
C: B1 .2: Identify personal skills, interests, and abilities and relate them to current career choice
C: B1 .3: Demonstrate knowledge of the career planning process
C: B1 .4: Know the various ways in which occupations can be classified
C: B1 .5: Use research and information resources to obtain career information
C: B1 .6: Learn to use the internet to access career planning information
C: B1 .7: Describe traditional and nontraditional career choices and how they relate to career choice.
C: B1 .8: Understand how changing economic and societal needs influence employment trends and future training.

C: B2: Identify Career Goals

C: B2 .1: Demonstrate awareness of the education and training needed to achieve career goals
C: B2 .2: Assess and modify their educational plan to support career
C: B2 .3: Select course work that is related to career interests
C: B2 .4: Maintain a career planning portfolio

Standard C: **Students will understand the relationship between personal qualities, education, training, and the world of work**

C: C1: Acquire knowledge to Achieve Career Goals

C: C1 .1: Understand the relationship between educational achievement and career success
C: C1 .2: Explain how work can help to achieve personal success and satisfaction
C: C1. 3: Identify personal preferences and interests which influence career choice and success
C: C1 .4: Understand that the changing workplace requires lifelong learning and acquiring new skills
C: C1 .5: Describe the effect of work on lifestyle
C: C1 .6: Understand the importance of equity and access in career choice
C: C1 .7: Understand that work is an important and satisfying means of personal expression

C: C2: Apply Skills to Achieve Career Goals

C: C2 .1: Demonstrate how interests, abilities and achievement relate to achieving personal, social, educational, and career goals
C: C2 .2: Learn how to use conflict management skills with peers and adults
C: C2 .3: Learn to work cooperatively with others as a team member
C: C2 .4: Apply academic and employment readiness skills in work – based learning situations such as internships, shadowing, and/ or mentoring experiences

Personal Social Development

***Standard A:* Students will acquire the knowledge, attitudes, and interpersonal skills to help them understand and respect self and others.**

PS: A1: Acquire Self Knowledge

PS: A1 .1: Develop positive attitudes toward self as a unique and worthy person
PS: A1 .2: Identify values, attitudes and beliefs
PS: A1 .3: Learn the goal setting process
PS: A1 .4: Understand change is a part of growth
PS: A1 .5: Identify and express feelings
PS: A1 .6: Distinguish between appropriate and inappropriate behavior
PS: A1 .7: Recognize personal boundaries, rights, and privacy needs
PS: A1 .8: Understand the need for self – control and how to practice it
PS: A1 .9: Demonstrate cooperative behavior in groups
PS: A1 .10: Identify personal strengths and assets
PS: A1 .11: Identify and discuss changing personal and social roles
PS: A1 .12: Identify and recognize changing family roles

PS: A2: Acquire Interpersonal Skills

PS: A2 .1: Recognize that everyone has rights and responsibilities
PS: A2 .2: Respect alternative points of view
PS: A2 .3: Recognize, accept, respect and appreciate individual differences
PS: A2 .4: Recognize, accept, and appreciate ethnic and cultural diversity
PS: A2 .5: Recognize and respect differences in various family configurations
PS: A2 .6: Use effective communication skills
PS: A2 .7: Know that communication involves speaking, listening, and non – verbal behavior
PS: A2 .8: Learn how to make and keep friends

***Standard B:* Students will make decisions, set goals, and take necessary action to achieve goals.**

PS: B1: Self – Knowledge Application

PS: B1 .1: Use decision – making and problem – solving model
PS: B1 .2: Understand consequences of decisions and choices
PS: B1 .3: Identify alternative solutions to a problem
PS: B1 .4: Develop effective coping skills for dealing with problems
PS: B1 .5: Demonstrate when, where, and how to seek help for solving problems and making decisions
PS: B1 .6: Know how to apply conflict resolution skills
PS: B1 .7: Demonstrate a respect and appreciation for individual and cultural differences
PS: B1 .8: Know when peer pressure is influencing a decision
PS: B1 .9: Identify long and short – term goals
PS: B1 .10: Identify alternative ways of achieving goals
PS: B1 .11: Use persistence and perseverance in acquiring knowledge and skills
PS: B1 .12: Develop an action plan to set and achieve realistic goals

***Standard C:* Students will understand safety and survival skills.**

PS: C1: Acquire Personal Safety Skills

PS: C1 .1: Demonstrate knowledge of personal information (i.e. telephone number, home address, emergency contact)
PS: C1 .2: Learn about the relationship between rules, laws, safety, and the protection of rights of the individual
PS: C1 .3: Learn about the differences between appropriate and inappropriate physical contact
PS: C1 .4: Demonstrate the ability to set boundaries, rights and personal privacy
PS: C1 .5: Differentiate between situations requiring peer support and situations requiring adult professional help
PS: C1 .6: Identify resource people in the school and community, and know how to seek their help
PS: C1 .7: Apply effective problem – solving and decision – making skills to make safe and healthy choices

PS: C1 .8: Learn about the emotional and physical dangers of substance use and abuse
PS: C1 .9: Learn how to cope with peer pressure
PS: C1 .10 Learn techniques for managing stress and conflict
PS: C1 .11 Learn coping skills for managing life events
Legend: A:A-1. 1 = Academic Domain, Standard A, Competency I, and Indicator I.
Reprinted with permission from the American School Counselor Association

New York State Learning Standards

Health, Physical Education, and Family and Consumer Sciences

Standard 1: Personal Health and Fitness
Students will have the necessary knowledge and skills to establish and maintain physical fitness, participate in physical activity, and maintain personal health.

Standard 2: A Safe and Healthy Environment
Students will acquire the knowledge and ability necessary to create and maintain a safe and healthy environment.

Standard 3: Resource Management
Students will understand and be able to manage their personal and community resources.

Mathematics, Science, and Technology

Standard 1: Analysis, Inquiry, and Design
Students will use mathematics analysis, scientific inquiry, and engineering design, as appropriate, to pose questions, seek answers, and develop solutions.

Standard 2: Information Systems
Students will access, generate, process, and transfer information using appropriate technologies.

Standard 3: Mathematics
Students will understand mathematics and become mathematically confident by communicating and reasoning mathematically, by applying mathematics in real world settings, and by solving problems through the integrated study of number systems, geometry, algebra, data analysis, probability, and trigonometry.

Standard 4: Science
Students will understand and apply scientific concepts, principles, and theories pertaining to the physical setting and living environment and recognize the historical development of ideas in science.

Standard 5: Technology
Students will apply technological knowledge and skills to design, construct, use, and evaluate products and systems to satisfy human and environmental needs.

Standard 6: Interconnectedness: Common Themes
Students will understand the relationships and common themes that correct mathematics, science, and technology and apply the themes to these and other areas of learning.

Standard 7: Interdisciplinary Problem Solving
Students will apply the knowledge and thinking skills of mathematics, science, and technology to address real life problems and make informed decisions.

English Language Arts

Standard 1: Language for Information and Understanding
Students will listen, speak, read, and write for information and understanding. As listeners and readers, students will collect data, facts, and ideas; discover relationships, concepts, and generalizations; and use knowledge generated from oral, written, and electronically produced texts. As speakers and writers, they will use oral and written language that follows the accepted conventions of the English language to acquire, interpret, apply, and transmit information.

Standard 2: Language for literary Response and Expression
Students will read and listen to oral, written, and electronically produced texts and performances from American and world literature; relate texts and performances to their own lives; and develop an understanding of the diverse social, historical, and cultural dimensions the texts and performances represent. As speakers and writers, students will use oral and written language that follows the accepted conventions of the English language for self-expression and artistic creation.

Standard 3: Language for Critical Analysis and Evaluation:
Students will listen, speak, read, and write for critical analysis and evaluation. As listeners and readers, students will analyze experiences, ideas, information, and issues presented by others using a variety of established criteria. As speakers and writers, they will use oral and written language that follows the accepted conventions of the English language to present, from a variety of perspectives, their opinions and judgments on experiences, ideas, information, and issues.

Standard 4: Language for Social Interaction:
Students will listen, speak, read, and write for social interaction. Students will use oral and written language that follows the accepted conventions of the English language for effective social communication with a wide variety of people. As readers and listeners, they will use the social communications of others to enrich their understanding of people and their views.

Languages Other Than English

Standard 1: Communication Skills
Students will be able to use a language other than English for communication.

Standard 2: Cultural Understanding
Students will develop cross – cultural skills and understandings.

The Arts

Standard 1: Creating, Performing, and Participating in the Arts
Students will actively engage in the processes that constitute creation and performance in the arts (dance, music, theater, and visual arts) and participate in various roles in the arts.

Standard 2: Knowing and Using Art Materials and Resources
Students will be knowledgeable about and make use of the materials and resources available for participation in the arts in various roles.

Standard 3: Responding to Analyzing Works of Art
Students will respond critically to a variety of works in the arts, connecting the individual work to other works and to other aspects of human endeavor and thought.

Standard 4: Understanding Cultural Contributions of the Arts
Students will develop an understanding of the personal and cultural forces that shape artistic communication and how the arts in turn shape the diverse cultures of past and present society.

Career and Occupational Studies

Standard 1: Career Development
Students will be knowledgeable about the world of work, explore career options, and relate personal skills, aptitudes, and abilities to future career decisions.

Standard 2: Integrated Learning
Students will demonstrate how academic knowledge and skills are applied in the workplace and other settings.

Standard 3a: Universal Foundation Skills
Students will demonstrate mastery of the foundation skills and competencies essential for success in the workplace.

Standard 3b: Career Majors
Students who choose s career major will acquire the career specific technical knowledge / skills necessary to progress toward gainful employment, career advancement and success in post secondary programs.

<u>Social Studies</u>

Standard 1: History of the United States and New York
Student will use a variety of intellectual skills to demonstrate their understanding of major ideas, eras, themes, developments, and turning points in the history of the United States and New York.

Standard 2: World History
Students will use a variety of intellectual skills to demonstrate their understanding of major ideas, eras, themes, developments, and turning points in world history and examine the broad sweep of history from a variety of perspectives.

Standard 3: Geography
Students will use a variety of intellectual skills to demonstrate their understanding of the geography of the interdependent world in which we live – local, national, and global – including the distribution of people, places, and environments over the Earth's surface.

Standard 4: Economics
Students will use a variety of intellectual skills to demonstrate their understanding of how the United States and other societies develop economic systems and associated institutions to allocate scarce resources, how major decisions – making units function in the United States and other national economies, and how an economy solves the scarcity problem through market and non-market mechanisms.

Standard 5: Civics, Citizenship, and Government
Students will use a variety of intellectual skills to demonstrate their understanding of the necessity for establishing governments; the governmental system of the United States and other nations; the United States Constitution; the basic civic values of American constitutional democracy; and the roles, rights, and responsibilities of citizenship, including avenues of participation.

LESSONS

Lesson 1: Making Effective Decisions

Name: Barbara Werner
Grades: 9 – 12

National Standards:
Academic Standard A: Students will acquire the attitudes, knowledge, and skills that contribute to effective learning in school and across a life span.
Academic Standard B: Students will complete school with the academic preparation essential to choose from a wide range of substantial postsecondary options, including college.
Personal/Social Standard B: Students will make decisions, set goals, and take necessary action to achieve goals.
Personal/Social Standard C: Students will understand safety and survival skills.

NYS Standards:
Career Development and Occupational Studies: Standard 1: Career Development
English Language Arts Standard 1: Language for Information and Understanding

Resources: Attached material

Lesson plan/procedure:

1. Provide students with the Decision Making Technique handout.
2. Briefly run through a simple decision utilizing the format presented on the handout. Example: "Challenge" – What to wear that day "Options" – Other clothing consideration "Considerations" – One outfit was not clean, one was nice, etc.
   "Option Selection" – The outfit they are wearing
   "Evaluation" – Did they make a wise choice?
3. Have students evaluate a decision they made in the past by filling out the handout. Direct them to
   write the problem or decision in the "Challenge" section. In the "Options" sections, they are to put alternatives they considered. They are to weigh the pros and cons for each option under

"Considerations." They should then note the decision they made and evaluate whether they made
a good one.

4. Discuss the following: How did it feel to write the steps out? Did it help them to break down the procedure and clarify the pieces to consider? How do they usually make decisions?
   Are they impulsive or do they carefully weigh their alternatives? Do they consider consequences? Looking back, did they make a wise decision with the situation they previously dealt with? What could they have done differently?
5. Give each student another copy of the handout. Have them complete the handout to work through a decision or challenge they are currently dealing with.

Evaluation: Students will demonstrate their learning based on group discussion.

Decision Making Technique

Challenge:

Option #1:

Considerations

****
Option #2:

Considerations:

****
Option #3:

Considerations:

****
Option Selection: Option #:

Lesson 2: Gaining Self-Awareness

Name: Paula Curci

Grades: 9 – 10

National Standards:
Academic Standard A: Students will acquire the attitudes, knowledge, and skills that contribute to effective learning in school and across a life span.
Career Standard A: Students will acquire the skills to investigate the world of work in relation to knowledge of self and to make informed career decisions.
Career Standard B: Students will employ strategies to achieve future career goals with success and satisfaction.
Career Standard C: Students will understand the relationship between personal qualities, education, training, and the world of work.
Personal/Social Standard A: Students will acquire knowledge, attitudes, and interpersonal skills to help them understand and respect self and others.

NYS Standards:
Career Development and Occupational Studies: Standard 1: Career Development
The Arts Standard 1: Creating, Performing, and Participating in the Arts
English Language Arts Standard 4: Language for Social Interaction

Resources: Students' "Demonstration Pieces"

Lesson plan/procedure:

1. Request that students in your group bring in a special something that they would like to show off. The item they bring in must represent something they have made (e.g. artwork) or done that they are proud of, a talent they posses, or an activity in which they participate.
2. Give each student a few minutes to talk about his or her special talent or moment.
3. Students who wish to can demonstrate their talent (e.g. dance) or share a piece of artwork or photograph of a special moment with the group.

4. Discuss with students:
    A. How did they feel while participating in their activity or hobby?
    B. What other talents do they have?
    C. How does having this talent make them feel?
    D. Are there any other hobbies or things they would like to accomplish? What is stopping them?
    E. What is self – concept? What part does being unique and your accomplishments play in the development of a positive self – concept? What else has impact on self – esteem?

Evaluation: Counselor will assess students' level of understanding based on group discussion.

Lesson 3: Resolving Conflicts

Name: Paula Curci

Grades: 9 – 10

National Standards:
Academic Standard A: Students will acquire the attitudes, knowledge, and skills that contribute to effective learning in school and across a life span.
Career Standard C: Students will understand the relationship between personal qualities, education, training, and the world of work.
Personal/Social Standard A: Students will acquire knowledge, attitudes, and interpersonal skills to help them understand and respect self and others.
Personal/Social Standard B: Students will make decisions, set goals, and take necessary action to achieve goals.

NYS Standards:
Career Development and Occupational Studies: Standard 1: Career Development
English Language Arts Standard 1: Language for Information and Understanding
English Language Arts Standard 4: Language for Social Interaction
Math, Science, and Technology Standard 5: Technology

Resources: Index cards, paper, pens, newspaper articles, lectern or podium (if available)

Lesson plan/procedure:

Pre - Activity Instructions:
As the facilitator, you will need to choose a topic you feel that the students are aware enough about through the media whether it is television, radio, newspapers, or the Internet.

Choose to split the students up into as many groups as may be able to represent several different points of view or positions on that issue as possible: i.e. Abortion = Group 1 – Pro – Choice –

Adamantly, Group 2 Anti – abortion for self, Pro choice for others, Group 3 Anti abortion adamant.

Write a point of view for each group on an index card. (Newspaper articles may be given to assist in the definition of each position assigned.)

Activity Instructions:

1. Instruct students to break into the necessary number of groups. Hand out point – of – view positions and inform groups to make the other groups aware of their position. Give articles if available.
2. Have groups assign someone to take notes and someone to speak for their groups.
3. Ask the groups to discuss the point of view on their card (and article) among themselves and to write arguments, statements, and debate points to support that position. (They must support the point of view assigned even if they do not personally agree.)
4. The speakers from each group must then address all of the students in the room as if they support that point of view.
5. After each group speaks, ask the students to discuss the following:
   - A. How did it feel to respect the ideals expressed by each group? Was it easy or difficult? Why?
   - B. How do we know if what each group said was the truth?
   - C. How do we go about dissecting all of the information given to us about a real life issue or social concern?
   - D. How do we balance our own values/positions with those of others?
   - E. How did it feel to go against our own feelings in each group?

Evaluation:
Counselor will discuss students' learning based on discussion of activity.

Lesson 4: Developing Relationship Skills through Labeling

Name: Paula Curci

Grades: 9 – 10

National Standards: *Personal/Social Standard A*: Students will acquire knowledge, attitudes, and interpersonal skills to help them understand and respect self and others.

NYS Standards: *English Language Arts Standard 4*: Language for Social Interaction

Resources: Magic markers, tape, pieces of paper or index cards marked with one stereotype on each (e.g., jock, nerd, bookworm, and gossiper.)

Lesson plan/procedure:

1. As students enter the room, tell them you would like to try an experiment and that the experiment requires that you tape a label on their back. Students should not try to find out what their label says.
2. After everyone is labeled, break the students into dyads.
3. Ask the students to begin a dyad discussion with each other referring to their partner as if he/she was the label on their back, e.g., LABEL: Bookworm – the partner may ask the bookworm how he/she liked the book being read in English class, etc. Other partners may speak to the Jock about an athletic event.
4. Switch to a different dyad groupings once or twice more.
5. Switch one more time, but this time, have students speak from the frame of reference as the label they believe is on their back.
6. After the experiment is over, ask the students if anyone has picked up on what their label is.
7. Have them remove the labels and check.

8. Ask for open discussion on: How it felt to be only referred to in one way? Did they find most people in the room discussed only certain topics or treated them in any particular way? Were they comfortable or uncomfortable with their label? (i.e. would they never want to be a bookworm? If so – why?)
9. Examine the assumptions people make about stereotypes.

Evaluation:
Counselor will evaluate students understanding of lesson through discussion.

Lesson 5: Developing Positive Attitudes and Making Healthy Choices

Name: Paula Curci

Grades: 9 – 12

National Standards:
Academic Standard A: Students will acquire the attitudes, knowledge, and skills that contribute to effective learning in school and across a life span.
Academic Standard C: Students will understand the relationship of academics to the world of work, and to life at home and in the community.
Career Standard A: Students will acquire the skills to investigate the world of work in relation to knowledge of self and to make informed career decisions.
Personal/Social Standard A: Students will acquire knowledge, attitudes, and interpersonal skills to help them understand and respect self and others.

NYS Standards:
Career Development and Occupational Studies: Standard 1: Career Development
English Language Arts Standard 4: Language for Social Interaction
Health, Physical Education, and Family and Consumer Sciences Standard 2: A Safe and Healthy Environment

Resources: Weekly reminder calendars (Make sure the weekly calendar has the time listed in ½ hour increments.)

Lesson plan/procedure:

1. Have students fill out each day of their life, ½ hour by ½ hour on the calendar, i.e. Monday 6:00 a.m. – wake up and take a shower; 6:30 a.m. – eat breakfast; 7:00 a.m. – get the bus. Have students finish their day noting all activities up until the time they go to sleep at night.
2. Have them do this for an entire week.
    A. Discuss the effective use of each student's time.

B. Do they utilize their talents and strengths during the week?
C. Are they overtaxing themselves with their schedules or underutilizing their time?
D. Discuss how to balance activities in order to get the best performance of their health and abilities.

Evaluation: Counselor will determine students' understanding of time management through discussion.

Lesson 6: Exploring the Concept of Trust

Name: Bob Germino

Grades: 9 -12

National Standards:
Academic Standard A: Students will acquire the attitudes, knowledge, and skills that contribute to effective learning in school and across a life span.
Career Standard C: Students will understand the relationship between personal qualities, education, training, and the world of work.
Personal/Social Standard A: Students will acquire knowledge, attitudes, and interpersonal skills to help them understand and respect self and others.
Personal/Social Standard B: Students will make decisions, set goals, and take necessary action to achieve goals.

NYS Standards:
Health, Physical Education, and Family and Consumer Sciences Standard 1: Personal Health and Fitness
Health, Physical Education, and Family and Consumer Sciences Standard 2: A Safe and Healthy Environment
Health, Physical Education, and Family and Consumer Sciences Standard 3: Resource Management
English Language Arts Standard 1: Language for Information and Understanding

Resources: Blindfold

Lesson plan/procedure:

1. Blindfold players and lead them in a part of the woods that has previously been roped off. The participants will use this rope as a guide and verbally and physically help the entire group to get through the trial.

2. Discuss how it felt not to know where you were going. How did it feel to have to trust someone other than yourself?
3. This activity can help us to realize that there are many people who trust us and whom we trust. In addition, the activity can make us more sensitive to the needs of others, and how to work cooperatively.

Evaluation:
Counselor will discuss activity and assess students' understanding through group discussion.

Lesson 7: Understanding How to Work Within a Community

Name: Bob Germino

Grade: 9 – 12

National Standards:
Academic Standard A: Students will acquire the attitudes, knowledge, and skills that contribute to effective learning in school and across a life span.
Career Standard A: Students will acquire the skills to investigate the world of work in relation to knowledge of self and to make informed career decisions.
Personal/Social Standard A: Students will acquire knowledge, attitudes, and interpersonal skills to help them understand and respect self and others.

NYS Standards: *Career Development and Occupational Studies: Standard 3a*: Universal Foundation Skills
Health, Physical Education, and Family and Consumer Sciences Standard 2: A Safe and Healthy

Resources: Several balls

Lesson plan/procedure:

1. Have players stand in a circle. Have several balls available. Players are to juggle a ball, throwing it to other members in the circle. Enter a second ball into the juggle, and another, keeping all balls in the air. Add in as many balls as the group is able to maintain.
2. Discuss what it took to successfully juggle. Who seemed most cooperative? What made them so?
3. This illustrates that everyone has an important place and role in a group. The goal is to develop good group feelings, cohesiveness and team spirit.

Evaluation:
Counselor will reinforce cohesion through group discussion.

Group Juggle

How to:
Have players stand in a circle. Have several balls available. Players are to juggle a ball, by throwing it to other members in the circle. Then, a second ball is entered into the juggle, and another, keeping all balls in the air.

Discuss:
Was it easy to figure out the game? Who seemed most cooperative? What made them so? Everyone has an important place and role in the group.

Objective:
To develop positive group feelings, cohesiveness, and team spirit.

An Alternative Exercise

Sneeches and Bips:

How to:
Designate participants as sneeches with one individual as the exception. This exception is designated as the bip. Tell the participants that they are all sneeches who must reach out and become the bip. The rules are that they must remain blindfolded, sneeches can only whisper the word sneech, and the bip can only whisper the word bip. As the participants mill around blindfolded, they whisper to each other their permitted word, in order to find the one participant that is the bip. When sneeches find the bip, they attach themselves to the bip, becoming the bip themselves. They then move on as a mass until all sneeches become bips and part of one big massive bip.

Discuss:
How did it feel to be a sneech? A bip? How many times did you feel like following the crowd? How many times did you feel left out?

Objective:
To become aware that it is okay to not follow the crowd. If you are uncomfortable with a situation, stay aware and away.

Lesson 8: Respecting Others (Session 1)

Name: Louis Bamonte & Gilbert E. Link

Grade: 9 – 12

National Standards:
Academic Standard A: Students will acquire the attitudes, knowledge, and skills that contribute to effective learning in school and across a life span.
Career Standard C: Students will understand the relationship between personal qualities, education, training, and the world of work.
Personal/Social Standard A: Students will acquire knowledge, attitudes, and interpersonal skills to help them understand and respect self and others.

NYS Standards:
English Language Arts Standard 1: Language for Information and Understanding
English Language Arts Standard 3: Language for Critical Analysis and Evaluation
English Language Arts Standard 4: Language for Social Interaction

Note: This lesson is in three parts.

Lesson plan/procedure:

1. Students are recommended for training by faculty via the faculty recommendation form. Faculty are encouraged to nominate students from diverse backgrounds.
2. Students are called together for a training session. The program is explained via the preparation sheet. An "ice – breaker" activity may be used to enable students to get to know others in the group.
3. Students are then asked to focus on an experience they have had where either they were the victim or victimizer in a prejudice situation. Examples of such experiences are given on the preparation sheet.
4. Students are asked to share their experiences in pairs.
5. Large group discussion follows with respect to how it feels to share such experiences.
6. Students are asked to take their story and develop it into a 2 – 3 minute "talk" for the next

session.

7. A date and time will be established for training session two.

Evaluation:
Counselors will assess understanding of concepts through discussing written assignment.

The Panel of Americans

Preparation Sheet

The Panel of Americans is a human relations group, which is sponsored by the National Conference of Christians and Jews. As such, the Panel's main focus is on an exploration of the diversity among Americans of different racial, religious, and ethnic origins. The Panel presents this diversity as a strength and as a source of richness in American life.

The group's basic activity is the Panel Presentation. These presentations are given by trained students from Copiague High School to various classes throughout the District. A typical panel presentation includes:

Five or six panelists speak for three minutes each. Each member has a prepared talk that focuses on aspects of his or her cultural, religious or racial background. Oftentimes, an experience of prejudice will be offered by the panelist and the feelings about this experience will be expressed with the hope of eliciting a response from the class.

After each panelist has presented, the moderator will conduct a discussion period in which he or she will attempt to have students in the "audience" react to and/or identify with the experience presented by the panel.

In order for the discussion period to "work," we suggest that you prepare your class for us the day before by focusing students attention on the ideas of prejudice, discrimination, and stereotyping. Perhaps a brief written assignment could be arranged centering on the children's experiences of prejudice and brotherhood in their own lives. Students in your class may also have a "story" to tell that in some way parallels the stories of Panel of Americans will share.

Some situations/experiences, which might be recalled and/or discussed by your students, include:

- Being a victim of prejudice
- Being an outcast/ "bothered" by other people
- Making someone else feel like an outcast
- Putting down someone of a particular religious, racial or cultural group by word or deed
- Being a minority in a particular situation
- Being a person who has friends from different racial, cultural, or religious groups
- Making an error about someone because you identified them with a particular group
- The effects of ethnic jokes
- A time when you tried to eliminate prejudice in your own life or in the lives of others

- An example of when being a member of a particular racial, cultural, or religious group seemed to be a positive thing (a strength)
- The reasons why people from different groups do not get a long and what can be done about it
- Having a handicap and being prejudiced against because of it

These are just some suggestions. You may have other ideas. There is no need to "cover all the bases." The idea is simply to get the students thinking so that they can share something with the panel.

Review Material on Human Relation Topics to Be Considered in Preparing Your Statement

- You share with the audience what it means as an individual to be a member of the panel and why you got involved.
- Who you are.
- Strong forces in your life.
- Can we change people, society, ourselves?
- Why has problem developed?
- What solutions will work?
- The role of peer pressure at all ages in society.
- What does it cost to have prejudice, discrimination, etc, thriving?
- What about our school, home, church, neighborhood, country, etc.?
- Is there strength in diversity?
- Are justice, acceptance, understanding, peace, happiness, respect just words?
- What about attitudes of friends, parents, etc.?

Guidelines:

1. Being honest and sincere is the best consciousness raising style.
2. Share your feelings, attitudes, beliefs, and hopes.
3. Look at the audience and be heard.
4. Use notes, but do not just read – pause and do not talk too fast.
5. You do not have to agree with fellow panel members or members of the audience.
6. Watch language – no profanity, slang, and jokes.
7. You have the freedom not to answer a question – remember you are not problem solvers – you are to open lines of communication by sharing views and feelings.

Lesson 9: Respecting Others (Session 2)

Name: Louis J. Bamonte & Gilbert E. Link

Grade: 9 - 12

National Standards: *Academic Standard A*: Students will acquire the attitudes, knowledge, and skills that contribute to effective learning in school and across a life span.
Career Standard A: Students will acquire the skills to investigate the world of work in relation to knowledge of self and to make informed career decisions.
Career Standard C: Students will understand the relationship between personal qualities, education, training, and the world of work.
Personal/Social Standard A: Students will acquire knowledge, attitudes, and interpersonal skills to help them understand and respect self and others.

NYS Standards: *English Language Arts Standard 3*: Language for Critical Analysis and Evaluation
English Language Arts Standard 4: Language for Social Interaction

Lesson plan/procedure:

1. Facilitator leads student in an "ice – breaker" activity so that students become reacquainted with one another.
2. Students are asked to share the "talk they have prepared." After 5 or 6 talks have been shared, the entire group will critique the talks they have heard thus far. The process continues until all have had a chance to share their talk.
3. The facilitator reviews the "panel process" (i.e. what actually happens in the classroom) and organized students into panels of 5 or 6 students, creating as much diversity in each panel as possible.
4. Arrangements are made for students to be present for and give a Panel of Americans presentation as per faculty request.

Evaluation:
Counselor will evaluate students understanding through presentations and discussions.

Lesson 10: Respecting Others (Session 3)

Name: Louis J. Bamonte & Gilbert E. Link

Grade: 9 - 12

National Standards:
Career Standard A: Students will acquire the skills to investigate the world of work in relation to knowledge of self and to make informed career decisions.
Career Standard C: Students will understand the relationship between personal qualities, education, training, and the world of work.
Personal/Social Standard A: Students will acquire knowledge, attitudes, and interpersonal skills to help them understand and respect self and others.

NYS Standards:
English Language Arts Standard 3: Language for Critical Analysis and Evaluation
English Language Arts Standard 4: Language for Social Interaction

Lesson plan/procedure:

1. Students are informed when and where the panel will be held. (Usually during a class period) It is recommended that each panel be gathered one day prior to their presentation for a brief review session.
2. The facilitator opens the sessions by explaining the process and the purpose of the Panel of Americans.
3. Each panel member then gives a "talk" based upon the following outline:
   A. Begin by stating your name and why you are a member of the Panel of Americans.
   B. State a theme or idea related to prejudice or stereotyping that you want to talk about (for example "I would like to talk to you about how ethnic jokes sometimes can get out of hand")
   C. Tell your story – be brief, real, sincere, and concrete.
   D. Wrap up your talk by re – stating (in different words) your original theme or idea.

E. After all panelists have presented, students in class are invited to share their own experiences, which may be similar to experiences shared by the panel. In this way, the members of the class and the panel interact.

Evaluation:
Counselor will assess understanding of respect through their "talk."

Your School Here
Guidance Department

Memo to:
From:
Re:
Date:

The Panel of Americans is a human relations group, which is sponsored by the National Conference of Christians and Jews. As such, the Panel's main focus is on an exploration of the diversity among Americans of different races, religious and ethnic origins. The Panel presents this diversity as a strength and as a source of richness in American life.

The group's basic activity is the panel. These presentations have been given by trained students from ______________________ to various classes in the high school. A typical "Panel Presentation" includes:

Five or six panelists will speak for 3 minutes. Each member has prepared talk which focuses on aspects of his or her cultural or racial background. Oftentimes, an experience of prejudice will be offered by the panelist and their feelings about this experience will be expressed with the hope of eliciting a response from the group.

After each panelist has presented their materials, the moderator, usually a faculty member, will conduct a discussion period in which he or she will attempt to have students in the audience react to and/or identify with the experience presented by the panel.
I have several requests:

1. I am interested in getting more faculty members involved with the Panel. If you are interested in becoming a moderator, please note this below.
2. I am interested in identifying present 10th or 11th grade students who could be trained as Panelists. You can use this space below to recommend such students.

Thank you for your help.

I would like to recommend the following 10th or 11th grade students as panelists for the Panel of Americans:

Students Name: **Homeroom Teacher**

I am interested in becoming a faculty moderator for the Panel of Americans:
Name:__________________________________**Free Period**___________________

Lesson 11: Understanding How Community Relates to One Another

Name: Bob Germino & Kathy McNally

Grades: 9 -12

National Standards:
Academic Standard A: Students will acquire the attitudes, knowledge, and skills that contribute to effective learning in school and across a life span.
Career Standard A: Students will acquire the skills to investigate the world of work in relation to knowledge of self and to make informed career decisions.
Career Standard C: Students will understand the relationship between personal qualities, education, training, and the world of work.
Personal/Social Standard A: Students will acquire knowledge, attitudes, and interpersonal skills to help them understand and respect self and others.

NYS Standards:
Career Development and Occupational Studies: Standard 1: Career Development
Health, Physical Education, and Family and Consumer Sciences Standard 2: A Safe and Healthy Environment
English Language Arts Standard 4: Language for Social Interaction

Resources: Paper

Lesson plan/procedure:

1. Have each student write a positive personal characteristic about himself or herself.
2. With the group, discuss acceptance of our positive traits, how we can celebrate our strengths, and how we can complement one another as we work together.
3. Discuss acceptance of self and others and about friendship and cooperation.

Evaluation:
Counselor will evaluate understanding through group discussion.

Lesson 12: Understanding Different Frames of Reference

Name: Bob Germino

Grade: 9

National Standards:
Academic Standard A: Students will acquire the attitudes, knowledge, and skills that contribute to effective learning in school and across a life span.
Academic Standard B: Students will complete school with the academic preparation essential to choose from a wide range of substantial postsecondary options, including college.
Career Standard A: Students will acquire the skills to investigate the world of work in relation to knowledge of self and to make informed career decisions.
Career Standard C: Students will understand the relationship between personal qualities, education, training, and the world of work.
Personal/Social Standard A: Students will acquire knowledge, attitudes, and interpersonal skills to help them understand and respect self and others.

NYS Standards:
English Language Arts Standard 1: Language for Information and Understanding
Health, Physical Education, and Family and Consumer Sciences Standard 2: A Safe and Healthy Environment

Lesson plan/procedure:

1. Divide group into dyads: Assign roles of stranger, homemaker alone, and neighbor.
2. Define situation: Stranger knocks on door; neighbor is watching. Homemaker answers door. Role play the situation.
3. Allow time: Participants need to discuss their feelings in this situation. Do not answer any questions regarding the situation; the participants must determine that for themselves.
4. **Discuss** Bring group together: Ask each stranger, homemaker and neighbor what happened. How did they feel? What did they think was going on?

Evaluation:
Counselor will evaluate understanding of feelings based on group discussion.

Lesson 13: Getting to Know Yourself

Name: Kathy McNally

Grades: 11 & 12

National Standards:
Academic Standard A: Students will acquire the attitudes, knowledge, and skills that contribute to effective learning in school and across a life span.
Academic Standard C: Students will understand the relationship of academics to the world of work, and to life at home and in the community.
Career Standard A: Students will acquire the skills to investigate the world of work in relation to knowledge of self and to make informed career decisions.
Career Standard C: Students will understand the relationship between personal qualities, education, training, and the world of work.
Personal/Social Standard A: Students will acquire knowledge, attitudes, and interpersonal skills to help them understand and respect self and others.
Personal/Social Standard B: Students will make decisions, set goals, and take necessary action to achieve goals.

NYS Standards
Career Development and Occupational Studies: Standard 1: Career Development
English Language Arts Standard 4: Language for Social Interaction

Resources: Attached questionnaire, business cards

Lesson plan/procedure:

1. Ask students to complete the questionnaire.

2. Conduct a follow up interview with students regarding questionnaire.

3. Encourage "on – going" communication with you by inviting students to your office. Give out business cards.

Evaluation:
Counselor will assess understanding of questionnaire based on individual responses.

Questionnaire

A: List on a separate paper all activities and jobs held during grades 9 -12, also include summer positions.

B: Answer the following questions to the best of your ability:

1. Name 3 specific strengths: academic and non – academic. Optional: describe each in 25 words.
2. Name and describe two personal weaknesses. How could these be viewed positively?
3. Name three adjectives that describe you.
4. What do you expect to be doing in ten years from now?
5. Describe your most important and gratifying experience.
6. What is unique about you?
7. What do you do in your spare time?
8. What do you consider the most important qualities in a friend?
9. If you could change one thing about your high school, what would it be?
10. What would you most like a college admissions committee to know about you?

Lesson 14: Freshman Orientation Groups

Name: Carl A. Torrillo

Grade: 9

National Standards:
Academic Standard A: Students will acquire the attitudes, knowledge, and skills that contribute to effective learning in school and across a life span.
Career Standard A: Students will acquire the skills to investigate the world of work in relation to knowledge of self and to make informed career decisions.
Career Standard C: Students will understand the relationship between personal qualities, education, training, and the world of work.
Personal/Social Standard A: Students will acquire knowledge, attitudes, and interpersonal skills to help them understand and respect self and others.

NYS Standards:
Career Development and Occupational Studies: Standard 1: Career Development
English Language Arts Standard 1: Language for Information and Understanding

Resources: See attached questionnaire

Lesson plan/procedure:

1. Counselor sends for 9th grade students in small groups of six to eight. The purpose of the meeting is to introduce students to the School Counseling Office and to provide an initial "get acquainted" session with their counselor.
2. Their counselor greets each student and makes a point of getting to know the individual's name, perhaps by providing nametags and by introducing the students to each other. An icebreaker activity might help.
3. The counselor stresses how students can utilize the Counseling Center and the desire of the counselor to establish rapport with the students. (Students need to feel comfortable here and to be able to depend on their counselor.) Explain how you will be assisting students and how knowing them well will be advantageous.

4. The counselor gets "feedback" from the students as to why it is important for a student to know his or her counselor well.

5. The attached questionnaire is distributed, and students spend the remainder of the time completing it. Counselor offers explanations as needed. The form is collected near the end of the meeting.

Evaluation:
Counselor will discuss certain questions on the questionnaire and evaluate students' understanding of lesson.

Freshman Questionnaire

Confidential

Directions: The questions on this inventory should be answered as completely as possible. They will be read only by your counselor to help get to know you better.

Name:

Nickname, If any:

Father's name and occupation:

Mother's name and occupation:

Names and ages of siblings:

Who lives at home with you?

What activities, games, and hobbies do you enjoy most outside of school?

Which school activities and/or sports so you plan to pursue?

What concerns, if any, do you have about your first year of high school?

Where is a favorite place, somewhere you feel most comfortable?

Where do you best like to be?

What is your least favorite place?

How would you rate your own level of self – esteem? High? Low? Need a boost? (Write one sentence)

What makes you proud? List two things that make you proud of yourself.

What do you think your parents expect of you this year?

How would your best friend describe you?

What else would you add about yourself that you would like me to know?

Complete these sentences:

I get lonely when

I get angry if

I cannot stand people who

I get frustrated when

I obey rules because

Someday I will be

If I could create a perfect world, I would

Whom do you admire?

We all look up to someone – even try to imitate them. List the people you admire most, then ask yourself why? How can you make these same qualities work for you?

People I Admire: Because:

Lesson 15: Applying Effective Study and Test Taking Skills

Name: Louis J. Bamonte

Grades: 9 & 10

National Standards:
Academic Standard A: Students will acquire the attitudes, knowledge, and skills that contribute to effective learning in school and across a life span.
Academic Standard B: Students will complete school with the academic preparation essential to choose from a wide range of substantial postsecondary options, including college.
Personal/Social Standard B: Students will make decisions, set goals, and take necessary action to achieve goals.

NYS Standards:
Career Development and Occupational Studies: Standard 1: Career Development
English Language Arts Standard 1: Language for Information and Understanding
English Language Arts Standard 4: Language for Social Interaction

Resources: As per below

Lesson plan/procedure:

1. Each counselor identified students (principally 9th and 10th graders) from their caseloads who are presently failing two or more subjects. Form two or three groups per counselor.

2. A minimum of three group sessions for each group should be scheduled in the school counseling office or conference room. This setting is motivational in that it affords students the opportunity to recognize and focus upon college and career resources, as well as participate in an academic improvement program.

3. The sessions revolve around issues such as:

   - How satisfied were you with your last report card?
   - In what ways do you wish to improve?
   - What assistance do you need to become a better student?

- Why become a better student? What is in it for you?
- How do your goals (short term & long term) relate to your study strategies now?
- How does your self – esteem relate to your performance as a student?

These sessions also include a discussion videotape entitled "The Study Game" which features Joe Montana, Chris Evert, Wayne Gretzky, Dr. Sally Ride, George Plimpton, Dr. Robert Ballard and Marva Collins discussing in a lively format various study strategies that will help students realize their true potential. Among the topics are

- Setting Goals
- Time Management
- Using Resources
- Procrastination Pitfalls
- Reading Strategies
- Memory Techniques
- Test Taking

Examples of materials utilized follow.

Evaluation:
Counselor will assess students' understanding through group discussion

Copiague High School
Guidance Department

Resources:

The Study Game (Videotape) High School Edition
Lessonware
5495 Belt Line Road, Ste. 120
Dallas, Texas 75240

Facilitating Study Skills Groups
Barbara J. Reisner
10240 West National Avenue
Suite 1900
West Allis, WI 53227

Becoming a Master Student
By David Ellis
College Survival
P.O. Box 8306
Rapid City, SD 57709 – 8306

Stop Studying, Start Learning by Richard Fenker
Tangram Press
5608 Malvey Avenue
Fort Worth, Texas

Study Skills Strategies by Velaine Lengefeld
Crisp Publications
Los Altos, California

Countdown to College by Zola Dinan Schneider & Phyllis V. Kalb
The College Board
45 Columbus Avenue
New York, New York 10023 – 6992

Where There's a Will, There's an A
By Claude Olney

Copiague High School
Guidance Department

References

Anderson, Sexton and Charles Anderson. (1992). Study Skills Made Easy. *The School Counselor, 39.*

Blum, Dorothy and L. Adelle Jones. (1993). Academic Growth Group and Mentoring Program for Potential Dropouts, *The SchoolCounselor,40.*

Heacox, Diane. (1991). *Up from underachievement*, Minneapolis Free Spirit Publishing.

Marshall, David. (1984). Study skills: Their values and why they should be taught, *NASSP Bulletin.*

Marten, Donald. (1998). *How to be a successful student*, San Anselmo, CA, Martin Press.

Thompson, Edward. (1987).The Yaggottaawanna Group: Improving Student Self– Perceptions Through Motivational Teaching of Study Skills, *The School Counselor.*

Wilson, Natalie. (1986). Preparing for Examinations: A Classroom Guidance Unit, *The School Counselor, March.*

By Dr. Louis J. Bamonte

Lesson 16: Four Year High School Planning/ or Graduation Work Sheet

Name: Sewanhaka High School & Half Hollow Hills High School West

Grades: 9 -12

National Standards:
Academic Standard B: Students will complete school with the academic preparation essential to choose from a wide range of substantial postsecondary options, including college.
Career Standard B: Students will employ strategies to achieve future career goals with success and satisfaction.

NYS Standards:
Career Development and Occupational Studies: Standard 1: Career Development
English Language Arts Standard 1: Language for Information and Understanding
Career Development and Occupational Studies: Standard 3b: Career Majors

Resources: Your 4 year Academic Planning Chart

Lesson plan/procedure:

1. Review transcript.

2. Review standardized test scores and career interest inventories.

3. Review High School curriculum as it may pertain to a particular career interest. For example, will student pursue regents or regents with advanced distinction?

4. Review sequence requirements and discuss with student whether he/she is aware of the various options available.

5. Based on discussion of above-mentioned activities, have student fill in academic planning chart.

6. Re-evaluate student's growth and progress as needed.

Evaluation:
Counselor will assess students' understanding of plan through discussions.

Lesson 17: Self-Evaluation Exercise

Name: Irene Balodimas

Grades: 9 & 10

National Standards:
Academic Standard C: Students will understand the relationship of academics to the world of work, and to life at home and in the community.
Career Standard A: Students will acquire the skills to investigate the world of work in relation to knowledge of self and to make informed career decisions.
Career Standard C: Students will understand the relationship between personal qualities, education, training, and the world of work
Personal/Social Standard A: Students will acquire knowledge, attitudes, and interpersonal skills to help them understand and respect self and others.

NYS Standards:
Career Development and Occupational Studies: Standard 1: Career Development
Career Development and Occupational Studies: Standard 3b: Career Majors
English Language Arts Standard 4: Language for Social Interaction

Resources: Attached

Lesson plan/procedure:

1. Hand out attached self – evaluation sheet to student during individual counseling session.

2. Encourage student to be honest in filling out evaluation sheet.

3. Have student identify areas of strengths and weaknesses.

4. Discuss relationship between ability levels and special interests.
   i.e., best marks in__________________ vs. my special abilities____________________.

Evaluation:
Counselor will determine understanding of student through discussion.

Self Evaluation

Directions: Fill in the blanks to complete the sentences:

1. My dream job is

2. The job I'll probably have is _________________ because _______________________

3. My parents want me to become

4. The kind of work I am interested in at present is

5. I think I would like this occupation because

6. Other related occupations that interest me are

7. My educational plans are __________________________ for the following reasons

8. My overall academic average is around _________ %

9. My best marks are in

10. My lowest marks are in

11. My favorite subjects in school are

12. The subjects I like least are

13. I believe my special abilities are

14. Some jobs I have done at home are

15. Some activities I have enjoyed in school are

16. Activities I enjoy outside of school include

17. I think I am suited to be a ______________________ because

18. What impact will the society in which I live have on my education?

Lesson 18: Study Habits

Name: Denise Cannon

Grades: 9 & 10

National Standards:
Academic Standard A: Students will acquire the attitudes, knowledge, and skills that contribute to effective learning in school and across a life span.
Academic Standard B: Students will complete school with the academic preparation essential to choose from a wide range of substantial postsecondary options, including college.
Academic Standard C: Students will understand the relationship of academics to the world of work, and to life at home and in the community.
Career Standard A: Students will acquire the skills to investigate the world of work in relation to knowledge of self and to make informed career decisions.
Personal/Social Standard B: Students will make decisions, set goals, and take necessary action to achieve goals.

NYS Standards:
Career Development and Occupational Studies: Standard 1: Career Development
Career Development and Occupational Studies: Standard 3b: Career Majors
English Language Arts Standard 1: Language for Information and Understanding
English Language Arts Standard 4: Language for Social Interaction
Math, Science and Technology Standard 5: Technology

Resources: Idea Box Handout

Lesson plan/procedure:

1. Hand out study habit inventory.

2. Discuss the need for students to understand their styles of learning and study habits that affect their performance.

3. Have students check off their answers to the study habits questionnaire.

4. Have students openly discuss and brainstorm ways in which they can improve on their study skills. Review study skills. Review discussion questions.

Optional Idea:

This questionnaire can be used in study halls, special education groups, or individually.

Evaluation: Counselor will determine students' understanding of activity through group discussions.

Study Skills Counseling

I. Student's Current Status

A. How does the student study?

1. Discuss student's current study techniques.

2. Discuss time, place and frequency of study time.

3. Evaluate student's strengths and weaknesses.

B. Administer Study Skills Inventory

1. Review inventory together.

2. Ask student to indicate the techniques that do work.

3. Identify techniques that do not work.

II. Suggest Successful Study Techniques

A. Organization Chart

B. Assignment Calendar

C. Time Schedule

Idea Box
Study Habits Inventory

Many successful teachers of study skills start the school year, course, or semester by having students complete a Study Habits Inventory such as the one suggested below. They use the information in planning lessons and programs and as the basis for individual conferences. They say it is the first step in getting a study skills program off the ground.

	Hardly Ever	Sometimes	Frequently	Most Always
1. Do you follow a daily schedule?	___	___	___	___
2. Do you have a regular place to work or study?	___	___	___	___
3. Do you keep track of homework assignments in a book or log?	___	___	___	___
4. Do you keep a long-term schedule or calendar of tests, projects, reports etc.?	___	___	___	___
5. Do you plan weekly reviews?	___	___	___	___
6. Do you take class notes?	___	___	___	___
7. Do you keep a notebook?	___	___	___	___
8. Do you have a note taking system?	___	___	___	___
9. Do you study with friends?	___	___	___	___
10. Do you listen well in class?	___	___	___	___
11. Do you look up new words?	___	___	___	___
12. Do you keep track of new words you learn?	___	___	___	___
13. Do you use the glossary?	___	___	___	___
14. Do you underline in textbooks?	___	___	___	___
15. Do you outline reading assignments?	___	___	___	___
16. Do you skim assignments before reading them	___	___	___	___
17. Do you read tables, charts, and graphs?	___	___	___	___
18. Do you have a private shorthand system for taking notes?	___	___	___	___
19. Do you use the index of a book?	___	___	___	___
20. Do you use the card catalogue in the library?	___	___	___	___
21. Do you use the periodical index?	___	___	___	___
22. Do you organize papers before you write?	___	___	___	___
23. Do you do a first draft?	___	___	___	___
24. Do you proofread for spelling and punctuation errors	___	___	___	___

25. Do you study effectively?	___	___	___	___
26. Do you learn in school?	___	___	___	___
27. Do you get eight hours of sleep each night?	___	___	___	___
28. Do you get regular exercise?	___	___	___	___
29. Do you make good use of your mind?	___	___	___	___
30. Do you try to improve your study habits?	___	___	___	___

Lesson 19: Career Planning Library Activity/ Career Report

Name: Sewanhaka High School

Grades: 10 & 11

National Standards:
Academic Standard B: Students will complete school with the academic preparation essential to choose from a wide range of substantial postsecondary options, including college.
Career Standard A: Students will acquire the skills to investigate the world of work in relation to knowledge of self and to make informed career decisions.
Career Standard B: Students will employ strategies to achieve future career goals with success and satisfaction.

NYS Standards:
Career Development and Occupational Studies: Standard 1: Career Development
Career Development and Occupational Studies: Standard 3b: Career Majors
English Language Arts Standard 4: Language for Social Interaction
Math, Science and Technology Standard 5: Technology

Resources: Career-Planning Worksheet

Lesson plan/procedure:

1. Review all interest inventory results in group or individual setting.

2. Have students choose an occupation of interest in which to investigate.

3. Review optional resources such as Dictionary of Occupational Titles, and Occupational Outlook Handbook. In addition, research computer programs designed to aid students in self – directed searches such as Expan, Discover, College Choice, and GIS.

4. Have students investigate trade magazines, want ads, yellow pages, and even the Internet.

5. Have students summarize the results of their career planning questions as outlined in Column 1 of Career worksheet utilizing the Career Report Outline.

Evaluation:
Counselor will evaluate student (s) understanding of career exploration through discussion, either in group or individually

Name: Date:

Career Planning Worksheet

Career Choice	Example: Actor/Actress	Career # 1
Career Explanation: **Resources:** Occupational Outlook Handbook Dictionary of Occupational Titles	Portrays role in dramatic production to interpret character or present characterization to audience. Rehearses part, lines. Comic; dramatic	
Career Requirements: Education? Experience? **Resources:** Occupational Outlook Handbook Yellow Pages Want Ads Trade Magazines	Suggest: Acting School, Talent, Endurance, Taking part in high school, college plays	
Who hires people in this career? Where do people in this career work or perform? **Resource:** Yellow Pages Want Ads Occupational Outlook Handbook	New York Stage Hollywood Local Drama guilds Traveling Shows Chicago, Miami	
How much is weekly pay in this career? Is there a future in this field? **Resources:** Occupational Outlook Handbook Want Ads Yellow Pages Is specialized experience or	Begin at around $200.00 per week. Join Union. Field is overcrowded now	

education needed for career? Will it take a long time to achieve this career goal? **<u>Resources:</u>** Expan, Discover, GIS and Coll. Choice Computer Prog.	Should look into acting school or specialized college. Get some local acting part in local theater. It could take a long time.	

Lesson 20: Quiz on Post High School Terminology for College Bound Student

Name: Nick Agostinacchio

Grade: 12

National Standards:
Academic Standard A: Students will acquire the attitudes, knowledge, and skills that contribute to effective learning in school and across a life span.
Academic Standard B: Students will complete school with the academic preparation essential to choose from a wide range of substantial postsecondary options, including college.
Career Standard A: Students will acquire the skills to investigate the world of work in relation to knowledge of self and to make informed career decisions.
Personal/Social Standard A: Students will acquire knowledge, attitudes, and interpersonal skills to help them understand and respect self and others.

NYS Standards:
English Language Arts Standard 1: Language for Information and Understanding
Social Studies Standard 1: History of the United States and New York

Resources: Questionnaire

Lesson plan/procedure:

1. Hand out 6-page questionnaire to students in senior homerooms.

2. Instruct seniors to fill out forms by an established deadline. Winners would be those who had a perfect score if handed in on time. Optional prizes to be awarded at school's discretion.

3. Optional ideas would be to hand them out during "Counselor Week," annual review or during college fair week. In addition, this activity could be used as a senior group exercise similar to a "Scavenger Hunt

Evaluation:
Counselor will assess understanding of college information by using the results of the test

Name the eight Ivy League Colleges
1.
2.
3.
4.
5.
6.
7.
8.

What does the acronym CUNY represent?

What does the acronym SUNY represent?

Where is the Crane School of Music?

Where are the Military Service Academies located?

What is the oldest college in the United States?

Where is Miami University?

Where are the four SUNY University Centers?

What is the oldest historical African American college in the U.S.?

List 12 colleges located in New York
1.
2.
3.
4.
5.
6.
7.
8.
9.
10.
11.
12.

What do the acronyms FAFSA and TAP represent?

In the world of financial aid, what does EFC represent?

What is the term ASVAB?

Who is/are the secretary/ies in the Guidance Department?

Who is/are the School Counselor/s at your school?

Based on new regulations, what are the new averages of the SAT I (verbal & math scores)?

In what grade level of high school does the average student take the PSAT?

What subject areas are tested on the SAT II test? List 6 only.
1.
2.
3.
4.
5.
6.

How may credits do you need to graduate from high school in New York State?

What is the name for B.O.C.E.S.?

List the members of your Board of Education.
1.
2.
3.
4.
5.

Who is the Coordinator for Curriculum at your high school?

Lesson 21: Personal and College Interviews

Name: Gina Crystal & Half Hollow Hills High School West

Grades: 11 & 12

National Standards:
Academic Standard B: Students will complete school with the academic preparation essential to choose from a wide range of substantial postsecondary options, including college.
Career Standard A: Students will acquire the skills to investigate the world of work in relation to knowledge of self and to make informed career decisions.
Personal/Social Standard A: Students will acquire knowledge, attitudes, and interpersonal skills to help them understand and respect self and others.
Personal/Social Standard B: Students will make decisions, set goals, and take necessary action to achieve goals.
Personal/Social Standard C: Students will understand safety and survival skills.

NYS Standards: *English Language Arts Standard 4*: Language for Social Interaction

Resources: Interview questions

Lesson plan/procedure:

1. Have students sign up for a mock interview. They should determine if it should be work related or college related.

2. Provide a modified list of mock questions to prep them (see attached questions).

3. Provide dos and don'ts of interviewing.

Evaluation:
Counselor will evaluate interviewing skills based on mock interview and through group or individual discussions.

The Interview

The following is a reprint from the Newsweek College Bound Newsletter:

An admissions officer at a small Midwestern school swears the following interviewing episode is factual:

The setting was not uncommon: Parents wait anxiously while son is interviews in an upstairs admissions office. Suddenly, dad suffers a heart attack and is rushed to the hospital. Left undisturbed, the interview proceeds. Son and admissions officer emerge later and mom fills them in on what happened to dad. She then quickly implores – get this "I trust this incident will not hurt my son's chances of being admitted."

Fact or folklore, this admissions tale underscores a need for perspectives, especially in the case of interviews. First, only about twenty percent of all four – year colleges require admissions interviews. Most of all, with a few exceptions, the interview is a relatively minor component in the application process.

A handful of schools use the interview to sell themselves to desirable students. More common is the evaluative interview where you will be challenged with questions to determine your strengths as a candidate. Finally, there is the less formal (and less intimidating) information interview that you will find at schools like Denison in Ohio. "We ask the student to discuss his credentials and hopefully indicate some awareness of self," says Admissions Director Richard Boyden. "At the same time, the student should use us as a resource for answering questions." In this case, the interviewer may write up his general impressions of you as a candidate or commemorate your meeting with nothing more than a handshake.

Skyrocketing travel costs and overworked admissions staffs make it unfeasible for most schools to require an on – campus interview these days. Alumni do the job for some schools at a local level. Required or optional, most administrators agree that the interview is one more chance to sell yourself – not to be passed up if manageable. "This is the only student credential that is not just a piece of paper," says Richard Skelton, Admissions Director at Bucknell. "It can personalize the admissions process and help us see a candidate more clearly."

How important is your interview? The smaller the institution the more vital it becomes. Says Lora Schilder, Associate Dean of Admissions at Hamilton College, "We want to learn how a student thinks, how he spend their spare time, what contributions he'll make to keep this place exciting and interesting. Hamilton is a very personal academic environment, so we take a very personal approach to admissions."

A few colleges actually make admissions decisions following an interview. But, the vast majority of schools, grades, class rank, test scores, and other references clearly take first priority, and the interview becomes more important only as a "nudge factor," says Denison's Boyden. "If we have a large group of students with comparable academic qualifications, then the interview can help with small distinctions."

As with other steps in the application process, you can call upon your school's college counselors for help in preparing for an interview. Remember you will want to do most of the talking during your meeting with an admissions officer or alumni representative – about your accomplishments, personal strengths, talents, and hobbies. Blow your own horn, but not too hard. In addition, get ready for the big question – Why do you want to attend the interviewer's school.

Relax, be yourself, and try to enjoy. Drop a note to your interviewer afterwards and you will stand tall (very few applicants ever get around to this important follow – up). Remember that the point of the interview is to help match the right student with the right school. It is not – do or die.

Suggestions for Personal Interview

In an interview, you naturally want to do all that you can to make a good impression on the interviewer. He/She can only know what you will tell him/her about yourself, by the way you look, act, and answer questions. Here is a brief summary of important reminders:

1. Dress neatly, and try to choose clothing that suits the situation.

2. Be on time. If you are late for an interview, the interviewer may decide that you are not really interested.

3. Know the college. This will enable you to show interest and ask relevant questions.

4. Greet the receptionist or the person who will introduce you to the interviewer. Be pleasant. Say your name clearly, and tell this person the name of the interviewer, if you know it.

5. Wait patiently if the interviewer is not ready for you.

6. Shake hands if it seems appropriate when you meet the interviewer. Use a firm handshake but not an overpowering one. You should wait for the interviewer to ask you to sit down.

7. Maintain eye contact with the interviewer during your time together. This is considered to be a sign of honesty and self – confidence. By the way, for this reason, it is better not to wear sunglasses during an interview.

8. Control any nervous behavior. Tapping your foot or clicking a ballpoint pen, for example, may annoy and distract the interviewer. Chewing gum is another thing you should not do during the interview.

9. Never smoke or smell like smoke.

10. Choose your words carefully and avoid slang or other special expressions that the interviewer may dislike or misunderstand.

11. Sit up in your chair. If your posture is good, the interviewer will see that you are alert and interested in what is happening.

12. Talk about what you do well. Often you will find that you can answer a question by mentioning certain talents, interests, or skills. Mention test scores only if you are asked to do so. If you have done poorly on a test, avoid making excuses for your performance. Deal with it in an honest, straightforward fashion.

13. Be clam. Try not to show disappointment or anger if you are not accepted, or if the interviewer does not make a decision immediately. They may have to see some other applicants before deciding.

14. Say "Thank – you." It is a good idea to drop a note to the interviewer thanking him/her for the opportunity to discuss you candidacy.

Arrange interview appointments far in advance of the desired date. Appointments are difficult to get, particularly at the very competitive colleges. It should be noted that in some cases, local alumni will conduct interviews in the community.

The Admissions Interview

Questions You May Be Asked:

1. Why are you considering this college?

2. What do you expect to be doing 10 years from now?

3. If you were the principal of your school, what would you change?

4. What do you have to bring to your school?

5. What newspapers and magazines do you read (Do not lie – be prepared to discuss issues that may be timely.)

6. What books not required in your courses have you read recently? (If it is trashy books, you might want to prepare something else – if it is science fiction or mysteries, admit it.)

7. If you could speak with any one living person, whom would it be, and why?

8. What television shows do you watch? (Do not fake it – be yourself)

9. How do you feel about Gun control, Prison reform, Nuclear power, and The use of drugs and alcohol?

10. What is the most important thing you have learned in high school?

11. What events have changed your life?

12. How would your best friend describe you?

13. What extra curricular activities have you found the most satisfying?

14. How do you spend the time after school?

15. What do you expect to get from your college experience?

You may or may not be asked some of these things, but it is a good idea to prepare. Role – play with a friend or parent acting as the interviewer, then reverse roles. Show by example how terrific you are. Even though you rehearse, you should be spontaneous and appear natural. Above all, listen to the interviewer. Be positive – be honest – be yourself – send a thank you note. Good Luck!

Questions to Ask

1. How many students in last year's freshman class returned for their sophomore year?

2. What procedure is used for class placement? (Important in areas of English and mathematics because freshman often vary significantly in their ability to handle these skills.)

3. How is the faculty advisor assigned? How is this done if the student is undecided about his/her major?

4. What kind of additional academic services does your college offer at no additional cost to the student (e.g., tutoring, counseling, study skills workshops, improving reading speed, etc…)

5. What percent of the student body lives on campus?

6. What are some of the activities planned for students on campus during weekends?

7. How are roommates selected if no preference is listed?

8. What are some of the rules and regulations that govern dorms? Are these co – ed halls?

9. What percent of your students received financial aid? What percent received scholarships based on academics? What percent of a typical financial aid package is in the form of a loan?

10. Is a room deposit is required, when is it due and when is it refundable?

11. If my family demonstrates financial need on the FAF or FFS forms, what percent of the need will typically be awarded and when can I expect to receive official notice of the award?

12. What is the typical size of a Freshman English class?

The College Visitation

The best way for you to learn about the educational program, faculty, facilities, atmosphere, and spirit of a college is to visit the campus, particularly when the college is in session.

College visits enable you to:

- Learn what college admissions expect from a candidate
- Evaluate the environment of the school (academic, physical, and social)
- Observe and talk with students who are attending and with whom you would associate

When to make the visit:

It is better to visit when the college is in session, so you will get a picture of the daily college routine. Spring of your junior year or fall of your senior year are most appropriate times to make a college visit. The summer provides an excellent opportunity for the entire family to visit. You do not have to apply to a college before you visit it.

What to look for:

- The size of classes
- The library facilities
- Strength of department you are likely to select as a major
- Are the laboratory facilities satisfactory?
- Composition of the student body
- Attractive dormitories – satisfactory study facilities
- Dining facility – quality of food
- Campus setting – beauty, orderliness and cleanliness
- What can you do when you want a snack?
- Adequate infirmary – the health services
- Religious facilities
- Facilities for leisure time – cultural programs – athletic facilities available – social life
- Do the college students appear to be happy, lively, and friendly?
- What is the attitude of the faculty toward the students?
- Were the students friendly and courteous toward visitors?
- Are the students serious and business – like toward their work

Suggestions:

- Telephone or write to the college admissions office to arrange for an interview.
- Ask the guidance secretary for an unofficial copy of your transcript several days before you leave for the interviews.
- Prepare for your visit by reading the catalog and having questions for your interviewer. In most cases, the purpose of an interview is for you to ask questions about the school and its programs rather than for the school to ask questions about you.

Lesson 22: Progress Review

Name: Nick Agostinacchio & Abby Hirsch

Grades: 9 & 10

National Standards:
Academic Standard A: Students will acquire the attitudes, knowledge, and skills that contribute to effective learning in school and across the life span.
Academic Standard B: Students will complete school with the academic preparation essential to choose from a wide range of substantial postsecondary options, including college.
Personal/Social Standard A: Students will acquire knowledge, attitudes, and interpersonal skills to help them understand and respect self and others.

NYS Standards:
Career Development and Occupational Studies: Standard 2: Integrated Learning
English Language Arts Standard 4: Language for Social Interaction

Resources: Progress report (academic & daily)

Lesson plan/procedure:

1. Review attached sheets and see if they meet your needs. If not, extract needed areas for review.

2. Inform students' teachers that the student may need individual attention in order for the forms to be filled out.

3. Have the student take the form from teacher to teacher either daily, weekly, or on any schedule you see fit.

Evaluation:
Counselor will evaluate students' progress with academics by follow through on the report.

Academic Progress

Please note your progress so far in each of your classes.

	I am Concerned	I am Doing Fine	I am Doing Well
English			
Social Studies			
Math (Which?)			
Science (Which?)			
Foreign Language			
Electives			

If there is something you need to see your counselor about immediately, check here ____ and write down some of your free periods and lunch:

Free periods____ Lunch period ____ Days ____

Name____ Date__________________

Counselor____

Daily Report
Guidance Department

Date______________________________ Counselor____________________________

Student____________________________ Teacher______________________________

Subject	Attendance	Effort	Attitude	Mark	Teacher

____ Have each teacher complete and sign

____Take it home for your parent/guardian to sign

____Return report to counselor

____
Parent/Guardian Signature

Remarks by teacher about the improvement the student is showing and suggestions for further improvement:

Lesson 23: Applying Effective Study and Test Taking Skills

Name: Half Hollow Hills High School West

Grade: 11

National Standards:
Academic Standard A: Students will acquire the attitudes, knowledge, and skills that contribute to effective learning in school and across the life span.
Career Standard B: Students will employ strategies to achieve future career goals with success and satisfaction.
Career Standard C: Students will understand the relationship between personal qualities, education, training, and the world of work.
Personal/Social Standard A: Students will acquire the knowledge, attitudes, and interpersonal skills to help them understand and respect self and others.
Personal/Social Standard B: Students will make decisions, set goals, and take necessary action to achieve goals.

NYS Standards:
English Language Arts Standard 1: Language for Information and Understanding
Career Development and Occupational Studies: Standard 3a: Universal Foundation Skills

Resources: See Options Sheet

Lesson plan/procedure:

1. Review suggested guidelines for an autobiographical sketch and its importance.

2. Review topics for discussion as possible autobiographical themes.

3. Have students attempt to draw up a sketch.

4. Be sure students understand the value of the autobiography.

5. Suggest that a rough draft be completed before the final copy is submitted. Encourage that it be proofread.

Suggestion:
Try to team up with the English department to accomplish this procedure. A cooperative inter – disciplinary approach will pay dividends.

Evaluations:
Counselor will evaluate student's autobiography through finished product.
Optional Guidelines for an Autobiographical Sketch

1. Discuss your immediate family background
   - A. Brothers and sisters, parents, guardians
   - B. Education and kinds of employment of family members
   - C. Special interests

2. In what activities have you been involved in, in the past 5 years?
   - A. School or extracurricular
   - B. Work
   - C. Community
   - D. Church or Temple
   - E. Summer program

3. What do you consider your most important achievement to date?
   - A. Academic
   - B. Personal
   - C. Social or community

4. How do you use your leisure time?
(Travel, special interests, home, etc.)

5. What are your plans for the next five years?
   - A. Educational
   - B. Vocational
   - C. Personal

6. What school subjects have you excelled in or liked best – why?

7. How do you see yourself as a person? How does this compare with how you believe others see you?

The letter of recommendation developed by your counselor is a very important part of the application package. By providing your counselor with an autobiographical sketch as described on these pages, you are helping insure that important information about you will be highlighted.

An additional autobiographical sketch utilizing some of the above guidelines will give your counselor more detailed information about you as an individual. **This material should be given to your counselor by due date suggested to insure inclusion in the letter of recommendation.**

Autobiography

1. Colleges will often request autobiographical information in order to get a better picture of you as a person. Even if the college of your choice does not request this information in essay form, it is a good idea for you, at this time, to gather your thoughts about yourself. This will prove helpful to you in the future interview situation.

2. The best way to approach this task is to assume that you are being asked the question – a favorite amongst interviewers – "Tell me about yourself?" Assuming that this is your objective, construct an outline which, if followed would best fulfill your objective which is to give the best possible picture of you – your interests, aspirations, accomplishment, etc.

3. Below is a list of areas, which should be touched upon in an autobiography. It is not necessary to deal with these in the order they are listed. There are some topics that you may or may not wish to cover, or need to cover. Keep in mind that your objective is to come up with as good a picture of you as you possibly can. Try to be interesting, avoid rambling, and do not be afraid to be creative. In addition, since this is a written picture of you, the way in which you present it is extremely important. Poor sentences, spelling, and organization will not present you in a positive light.

Suggested Topics for Discussion:

1. Describe a pressing problem you have had to face in your life and how you dealt with it. What self-control were you able to exert? What did you learn from the experience?

2. Describe a personal experience in which you showed qualities of leadership. What happened that made you feel influential?

3. Describe something you have done that has given you satisfaction.

4. Where do you see yourself in ten years?

5. Select some school or other experience for which you have derived exceptional profit – describe it explaining its values to you.

Lesson 24: Applying Effective Study and Test Taking Skills

Name: Antonette Ursini & Anna Zurawinski

Grades: 9 – 11

National Standards:
Academic Standard A: Students will acquire the attitudes, knowledge, and skills that contribute to effective learning in school and across the life span.
Academic Standard B: Students will complete school with academic preparation essential to choose from a wide range of substantial postsecondary options, including college.
Career Standard B: Students will employ strategies to achieve future career goals with success and satisfaction.

NYS Standards:
Career Development and Occupational Studies: Standard 2: Integrated Learning
Career Development and Occupational Studies: Standard 3b: Career Majors
English Language Arts Standard 1: Language for Information and Understanding

Resources: See attached

Lesson plan/procedure:

1. See attached method and objective for career planning. Read carefully.

2. Follow instructions indicated on each page.

Evaluation:
Counselor will evaluate students' understanding of career activities through completion of exercise and through individual or group discussion.

Career Planning

Objective: To establish a guideline of guidance related assignments that students need to accomplish each year for personal effective career assessment.

Method: Use the blackboard to draw out a time line of activities that the students can follow from 9th grade on. Discuss that this is "self – work" to be done on their own with the help of their school counselor.

The following chart emphasizes the Career Guidance Activities used in each grade level to assist you in identifying your interests and abilities. It is necessary that you participate in these activities to make appropriate career decisions throughout your school life. In the blank spaces provided, fill in the scores and activity information that relates to you.

	Activities Chart	Getting on the Right Track
Grade	*School Tests and Activities*	*Career Guidance Activities*
7	Learning Styles Inventory	Career Center Use of Guidance Information System (GIS)
	Achievement Test:	Counselor Annual Review
	Reading Score________	Home Economics /Career Class
	Math Score________	Technology Class
	Extracurricular Clubs: ________________________ ________________________ ________________________ ________________________	Career Planning Folder

8	Aptitude Test:	Job – O Inventory
	Verbal Score___________	Career Day – Career Speakers
	Numerical Score_________	Home/Career/Technology Classes
	Mechanical Score___________	Art Class
	Abstract Reasoning Score______	Counselor Annual Review
	Extracurricular Clubs:	Career Filed Trips
	____________________________	
	____________________________	Career Center Orientation
	____________________________	
	____________________________	Newsletters
	____________________________	
		Career Planning Folder
9	Achievement Test:	Class Visitations
	Math Score________	Class Field Trips
		Career Days and Speakers
	Course sequences	Counselor Annual Review
	Electives	Career Center Use
	Extra Curricular Clubs:	Career Assemblies
	____________________________	
	____________________________	Newsletters
	____________________________	
	____________________________	
	____________________________	

	Community Service: ___________________________ ___________________________ ___________________________ ___________________________	
10	Preliminary Scholastic Aptitude Test: PSAT	Career Day
	Verbal Score_________	College Night
	Math Score_______	Counselor Annual Review
	Extra Curricular Clubs: ___________________________ ___________________________ ___________________________ ___________________________	Field Trips Career Center Use Newsletter
	Community Service: ___________________________ ___________________________ ___________________________	
11	Preliminary Scholastic Aptitude Test PSAT	Career Day
	Verbal Score_________	Career Speakers
	Math Score________	College School Visits
	College Entrance Exam-	College Fairs

Scholastic Aptitude Test:

Verbal Score_______ Career Center Use

Math Score______

Lesson 25: Interview Workshop

Name: Toni MacDonald

Grade Level: 11th & 12th

National Standards:
Academic Standard A: Students will acquire the attitudes, knowledge, and skills that contribute to effective learning in school and across the life span.
Academic Standard B: Students will complete school with the academic preparation essential to choose from a wide variety of substantial post-secondary options, including college.
Academic Standard C: Students will acquire the skills to investigate the world of work in relation to knowledge of self and to make informed career decisions.
Personal/Social Standard A: Students will acquire knowledge, attitudes, and interpersonal skills to help them understand and respect self and others.
Personal Social Standard B: Students will make decisions, set goals, and take necessary actions to achieve goals.

NYS Learning Standards:
Career Development and Occupational Studies: Standard 3a: Universal Foundation Skills
English Language Arts Standard 1: Language for Information and Understanding
English Language Arts Standard 4: Language for Social Interaction

Resources: Attached questions

Lesson plan/procedure:

Review all of the following questions with students when they are preparing interviews, primarily college interviews.

In advance ask for students to volunteer to tape mock interviews. Obtain parental permission. The videos can be used for future students to critique.

Evaluation:
The counselor will evaluate students' understanding of the interview process through modeling and role-playing.

<u>The College Interview</u>

I. What is an interview?

a. A chance to allow a potential college or university get to know you better, and vice versa.

b. The interview should be perceived as a chance for you to learn as much about a school as they learn about you.

c. It is part of the entire process of finding the school that is right for you. During the interview not only will the interviewer get to know you as a person, but also you will get a real feeling of the school through the interview.

II. Why should I have an interview? Don't school base their admissions on grades and SAT scores?

a. Everyone has a Rank-in-Class, SAT scores, achievement tests, etc., but not everyone takes the time and effort to see the schools to which they re applying and have an interview.

b. In fact, in many cases the interview can make the job of the admissions counselor much easier; trough the interview the counselor has a much better idea as to who you really are underneath you application. One might say the interview brings the application to life.

c. The interview is a perfect opportunity to explain trends in your transcript (e.g. My grades dipped in my sophomore year because I had mono). Or to explain something which may not be picked up as easily as a spotty high school record, such as an extenuating circumstances; trip abroad, summer job, athleticism.

III. How important is the interview?

a. The interview will be used as one of many factors in the admissions decision.

b. A good interview will not take the place of a spotty high school record, and a bad interview will not outweigh a good academic record.

c. The interview in most cases, cannot harm your chances for acceptance and will only be used to your advantage.

IV. Other types of interviews

a. Although the most common interview is the one with a professional admissions office not all schools are prepared to offer this kind. Some other types of interviews include:

1. The student interview
2. The alumni interview
3. Group interviews / information session
4. The audition
5. Special interest interview (athletic, musician, actor, etc)

V. How do I prepare for the interview? Suggestions:

a. Research the schools you will be interviewing with. Try to become familiar with the catalogue, admissions requirements, academic offerings, size of student body, etc. This will show the interviewer that you are well aware of what the school has to offer.

b. Dress appropriately!! This will mean different things to different people. For example, some may feel comfortable in a suit and tie, others may overdressed and uncomfortable dressed in a suit, this could effect the interview. "Dress appropriately" means to dress neatly, as you would if you were going to a job interview. Some people may feel as though they want to dress in a manner reflective of their personality, even if that means torn jeans and sneakers. The reality is that the interviewer will get to know the real you even if you dress neatly and more conservative. Keep in mind you want to make a good first impression.

c. Be on time.

d. Be polite. The interviewer will probably greet you with a friendly "Hello" and a firm handshake, reciprocate!

e. Be aware of your body language.

Posture
Eye Contact
Avoid crossing arms or anything that may be viewed as negative or disinterested

f. Ask questions when/where appropriate

g. Relax and Be Your Self! You will find that if you are honest with yourself and the interviewer, everything will fall into place and flow naturally. Don't try to impress the interviewer by stretching the truth or do something that may result in an embarrassing moment or an awkward silence.

VI. Keep in mind the fact that most interviewers are adept at facilitating conversation, in addition to knowing how to relax the interviewee. They will want the interviewer to be as successful as you do, because in part it is a reflection of them and the school. They will want you to leave feeling good about yourself and their school.

VII. Once you are home and have a chance to reflect on the interview, an appropriate gesture would be to write a short letter of thanks to the interviewer. You might mention how much you appreciated the time he/she spent with you, how relaxed you felt, etc.

VIII. What will be asked of me in an interview? Sample questions:

How did you learn about this college or university?
What has attracted you to this school?
What are you looking for in a school?
Have you seen the campus?
What do you feel you have to offer this school?
What are you aspirations?
Why do you want to go to this college?
What are you most proud of? Why?
Describe your high school?
What were your favorite /least favorite courses?
Have you worked to your potential?
Are there any extenuating circumstances that affect you high school performance?
How do you spend your summers?
What are your hobbies / interests?
What would you change about yourself, if anything?
What is the most difficult decision you've had to make?
Who have you been influenced by?
What three books would you take to a desert island?
If your home were on fire, and you only had 5 minutes to gather 3 items, what would you take and why?
What is your favorite movie?
What is the best book you have ever read?

IX. What questions should I ask?

a. First, remember that asking questions is essential. Some suggestions:

What are the students like here?
What do the students like most/least about the college?
What percentage of students are active in Greek life? What role do fraternities and sororities play on campus?
Is the campus safe? What are the security measures taken on campus?
What happens on the weekends?
How many students live on campus?
What role do athletics play on campus?
What are my chances of making a team?
What division athletics is played here?
What is the school's policy on alcohol and how strictly is it enforced?
Is housing guaranteed for 4 years?
Are freshman housed together?
What kind of food plans do you offer?
What are the computer facilities like on campus? Do they suggest you bring your own?
Do graduate assistance teach any classes?
What is the average class size?
What is the male/female ratio?
Are there any plans for expanding the campus or adding new programs in the future?
What percent of students receive financial aid? What is the average financial age package like?
What percent of freshmen return for sophomore year?

X. Summary

a. Although interviews may vary, the basic format is as follows:

Ice breaker / getting the students to relax and enjoy the visit
Talking about you and your high school experience
Talking about the college
Your questions
Meeting parents and answering their questions

b. The purpose of the interview is for you to get to know the school, and for them to get to know you.

c. An interview can only help you.

d. Be honest, be real, be yourself, and everything will be fine.

e. Good luck!!! Let us know how you do!

Lesson 26: Newspaper Cooperative

Name: Bob Germino and Kathy McNally

Grade Level: 9th – 12th

National Standards:
Academic Standard A: Students will acquire the attitudes, knowledge, and skills that contribute to effective learning in school and across the life span.
Academic Standard B: Students will complete school with the academic preparation essential to choose from a wide variety of substantial post-secondary options, including college.
Personal/Social Standard A: Students will acquire knowledge, attitudes, and interpersonal skills to help them understand and respect self and others.
Personal Social Standard B: Students will make decisions, set goals, and take necessary actions to achieve goals.
Career Standard A: Students will acquire the skills to investigate the world of work in relation to knowledge of self and to make informed career decisions.
Career Standard C: Students will understand the relationship between personal qualities, education, training, and the world of work.

NYS Learning Standards:
Career Development and Occupational Studies: Standard 2: Integrated Learning
Health, Physical Education, and Family and Consumer Sciences Standard 2: A Safe and Healthy Environment
English Language Arts Standard 1: Language for Information and Understanding
Mathematics, Science, and Technology Standard 5: Technology
Mathematics, Science, and Technology Standard 6: Interconnectedness

Resources: Old newspaper, rolls of masking tape

Lesson plan/procedure:

Create groups of approximately six people each. Provide about five inches in height of old newspaper and one roll of masking tape for each group.

Give each group 5-10 minutes to discuss how to build a shelter over themselves with paper and tape. No one can touch the materials while talking. Give 5-10 minutes to build their structure, also without talking.

Once finished, discuss the importance of team building and cooperation and how they are related to feeling good about ourselves. When we accomplish something while working well with others, we are given the opportunity to receive positive feedback and, in turn, feel good about ourselves.

Evaluation: Discuss with the students group process and evaluate effectiveness of lesson through group discussion.

Lesson 27: Understanding How Community Relates to Work

Name: Kathy McNally

Grade Level: 9th – 11th

National Standards:
Personal/Social Standard A: Students will acquire knowledge, attitudes, and interpersonal skills to help them understand and respect self and others.
Career Standard A: Students will acquire the skills to investigate the world of work in relation to knowledge of self and to make informed career decisions.
Career Standard C: Students will understand the relationship between personal qualities, education, training, and the world of work.

NYS Leaning Standards:
Career Development and Occupational Studies: Standard 1: Career Development
English Language Arts Standard 1: Language for Information and Understanding
English Language Arts Standard 4: Language for Social Interaction

Resources: Work values checklist and summary

Lesson plan/procedure:

Discuss with students the importance of considering their personal values when choosing a career. Discuss different examples of career and the values that are attached to them.

Have students fill out checklist. Explore additional values that may not be listed.

Ask students to complete the work values summary sheet and discuss how the "Very Important" values compliment or conflict each other.

Evaluation:
Discuss values with the students based on their checklists.

WORK VALUES CHECKLIST

Using the following scale to rate the importance of these work values to you:
VI = Very Important **SI** = Somewhat Important **NI** = Not Important

Chance for promotion, getting ahead	VI _____	SI_____	NI______
Travel and adventure	VI_____	SI_____	NI______
Being of service to others	VI______	SI______	NI______
Be involved in a variety of tasks or problems	VI_____	SI______	NI______
Earn respect and recognition	VI_____	SI______	NI______
Friendly co-workers	VI_____	SI______	NI______
Pleasant working conditions	VI_____	SI______	NI______
Expectations by boss clearly stated	VI_____	SI______	NI______
Flexible hours: control over own time	VI______	SI______	NI______
Regular hours (little overtime)	VI______	SI______	NI______
Working for an important cause	VI_____	SI_____	NI______
Chance to use my own ideas/ be creative	VI_____	SI_____	NI_____
Working as part of a team or group	VI_____	SI_____	NI_____
Being my own boss	VI_____	SI______	NI______
Living in a specific location	VI_____	SI_____	NI______
Working on one project at a time	VI_____	SI_____	NI______
Time and energy for leisure time	VI_____	SI_____	NI______

Opportunity to learn and experience new things	VI_____	SI_____	NI_____
Steady, secure income, even if small	VI_____	SI_____	NI_____
Big money, but uncertain	VI_____	SI_____	NI_____
Competitive, chance to make it big, take risks	VI_____	SI_____	NI______
A lot of responsibility	VI_____	SI_____	NI______
Being physically active	VI_____	SI_____	NI_____
Challenging work, opportunity to use special skills/knowledge	VI_____	SI_____	NI_____
Being the leader, having authority	VI_____	SI_____	NI_____
Working outdoors	VI_____	SI_____	NI_____
Working alone, by yourself	VI_____	SI_____	NI_____
Important, necessary work	VI_____	SI_____	NI_____

WORK VALUES SUMMARY

1. List those work values, which are Very Important (VI) to you.

2. Do you see any conflicts between two or three of these Very Important (VI) work values?

Lesson 28: Analyzing Skills and Interests

Name: Kathy McNally

Grade Level: $9^{th} - 11^{th}$

National Standards:
Academic Standard A: Students will acquire the attitudes, knowledge, and skills that contribute to effective learning in school and across the life span.
Academic Standard B: Students will complete school with the academic preparation essential to choose from a wide variety of substantial post-secondary options, including college.
Personal/Social Standard A: Students will acquire knowledge, attitudes, and interpersonal skills to help them understand and respect self and others.
Career Standard A: Students will acquire the skills to investigate the world of work in relation to knowledge of self and to make informed career decisions.
Career Standard B: Students will employ strategies to achieve future career goals with success and satisfaction.
Career Standard C: Students will understand the relationship between personal qualities, education, training, and the world of work.

NYS Leaning Standards:
Career Development and Occupational Studies: Standard 1: Career Development
Career Development and Occupational Studies: Standard 3b: Career Majors
English Language Arts Standard 1: Language for Information and Understanding
English Language Arts Standard 4: Language for Social Interaction

Resources: Vocational interest checklist and summary

Lesson plan/procedure:

Discuss with the students the importance of liking your job. Ask them to imagine what it would be like to spend the rest of their lives working in a job that they dislike. Ask them also to think about how different it would be to love your job and look forward to going everyday. This discussion should illustrate the value of knowing yourself and the kinds of activities that you like and enjoy. Are you a people person, the creative type, a team player, etc.

Have students fill out the checklist. When students are done, complete the summary together as a class. Discuss possible jobs and careers that compliment the various interest areas.

Evaluation:
Students will evaluate their skills and interests through discussion about their checklist.

VOCATIONAL INTEREST CHECKLIST

Listed below are a variety of work activities
Check **L** if you like the activity
Check **I** if you are indifferent (don't care)
Check **D** if you do not enjoy the activity
Check **H** if you have not tried it, but would like to

Activities:

1.Operating machinery	L___	I____	D___	H___
2. Playing a musical instrument	L___	I____	D___	H___
3. Raising plants/vegetables	L___	I____	D___	H___
4. Organizing cabinets or closets	L___	I____	D___	H___
5. Producing a specific product	L___	I____	D___	H___
6. Display merchandise in a store window	L___	I____	D___	H___
7. Building a wooden table or cabinet	L___	I____	D___	H___
8. Rearrange a room or stock shelves	L___	I____	D___	H___
9. Create an art object	L___	I____	D___	H___
10. Researching information about a subject	L___	I____	D___	H___
11. Making a speech	L___	I____	D___	H___
12. Develop a new school program or Community project	L___	I____	D___	H___
13. Making a chart based on statistics	L___	I____	D___	H___
14. Discussing politics or current events	L___	I____	D___	H___

15. Writing a report	L___	I____	D___	H___
16. Analyzing something you have read	L___	I____	D___	H___
17. Performing scientific experiments	L___	I____	D___	H___
18. Solving crossword puzzles or riddles	L___	I____	D___	H___
19. Attending lectures or speeches	L___	I____	D___	H___
20. Teaching or training others	L___	I____	D___	H___
21. Helping people solve their problems	L___	I____	D___	H___
22. Supervising other people	L___	I____	D___	H___
23. Interviewing people	L___	I____	D___	H___
24. Bargaining with people	L___	I____	D___	H___
25. Starting a conversation with a stranger	L___	I____	D___	H___
26. Being supervised by someone	L___	I____	D___	H___
27. Persuading someone to do something	L___	I____	D___	H___
28. Entertaining others	L___	I____	D___	H___
29. Listening to others	L___	I____	D___	H___

SUMMARY OF VACATIONAL INTERESTS

1. Total number of liked activities in numbers 1-10. These activities involve work with *objects and/or things.*

2. Total number of liked activities in numbers 1-20. These activities involve work with *ideas and/or knowledge.*

3. Total number of liked activities in numbers 21-29. These activities involve work with *people.*

4. What kinds of things do you like to work with: (ex: stamps, cars, stereo equipment, cooking equipment, etc.)?

   ____
   ____
   ____

5. What kinds of ideas do you like to read, discuss, or write about: (ex: music, politics, sports, art, human behavior, travel, etc.)?

   ____
   ____
   ____

6. What kinds of people do you like to work with: (ex: sick people, children, customers, elderly, athletes, etc.)?

   ____
   ____
   ____

7. How do you like to work with people: (ex: talk with them, do things for them, do things with them, etc.)?

   ____
   ____
   ____

Lesson 29: Preparing a Resume

Name: Kathy McNally

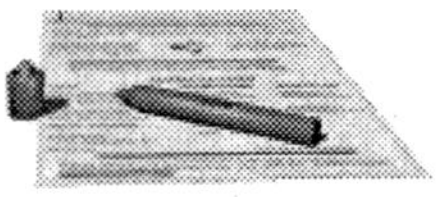

Grade Level: 12th

National Standards:
Academic Standard A: Students will acquire the attitudes, knowledge, and skills that contribute to effective learning in school and across the life span.
Career Standard A: Students will acquire the skills to investigate the world of work in relation to knowledge of self and to make informed career decisions.

NYS Learning Standards:
Career Development and Occupational Studies: Standard 3a: Universal Foundation Skills
Career Development and Occupational Studies: Standard 3b: Career Majors
English Language Arts Standard 1: Language for Information and Understanding
English Language Arts Standard 4: Language for Social Interaction

Resources: Resume hints worksheet

Lesson plan/procedure:

Discuss with students the importance of first impressions either in person or on paper. Ask if anyone has applied for a job and how they supplied information about themselves.

Talk about the kinds of things that belong in a resume and how to present these facts. Have students list the facts and activities that they would include in their own resume. Provide samples of good and bad resumes for students to review. The ultimate goal is for each student to produce a well thought out and complete resume of their own.

Note: This would be a good activity to do with the English teacher.

Evaluation: Counselor will evaluate students' understanding or resume writing through the results of students' writing.

RESUMES - HINTS

1. Appearance is important – no mistakes
   Typed
   Offset
   Watch margins

2. Use action words
   (Avoid – I, helped organize, worked with)

3. Avoid jargon

4. No abbreviations

I. Work History
   All jobs – paid/unpaid – dates
   What did you do?

II. Using job objective – organize format

   Name Telephone #
   Address
   Job title, where, dates
   Description
   Job title, where, dates
   Description

   Heading will vary based on the individual.

   A. Work Experience
   B. Extracurricular Activities
   C. Education

Lesson 30: Your Resume

Name: Bob Germino

Grade Level: 9th – 12th

National Standards:
Personal/Social Standard A: Students will acquire knowledge, attitudes, and interpersonal skills to help them understand and respect self and others.
Personal/Social Standard C: Students will understand safety and survival skills.
Career Standard A: Students will acquire the skills to investigate the world of work in relation to knowledge of self and to make informed career decisions.

NYS Leaning Standards:
Career Development and Occupational Studies: Standard 1: Career Development
English Language Arts Standard 1: Language for Information and Understanding

Resources: Paper, pen/pencils

Lesson plan/procedure:

Discuss with students the purpose of a resume: to communicate information about them to another person. It is a reflection of themselves, their personality, creativity and ability to express these thoughts.

Have participants write informally, in their own words, how they see themselves and how they want others to see them. Then have them rewrite the informal paper in a formal manner adding information that would be important to an employer or organization when applying for a job or membership.

Information should include: full name, address, telephone number, educational background, languages spoken, special skills, life or employment objectives, hobbies or special interests.

Evaluation:
Counselor will discuss resume writing with the students and evaluate their understanding through their writing.

Lesson 31: Researching a Career Field

Name: Bob Germino & Kathy McNally

Grade Level: 9th & 10th

National Standards:
Academic Standard A: Students will acquire the attitudes, knowledge, and skills that contribute to effective learning in school and across the life span.
Academic Standard B: Students will complete school with the academic preparation essential to choose from a wide variety of substantial post-secondary options, including college.
Career Standard A: Students will acquire the skills to investigate the world of work in relation to knowledge of self and to make informed career decisions.
Career Standard B: Students will employ strategies to achieve future career goals with success and satisfaction.
Career Standard C: Students will understand the relationship between personal qualities, education, training, and the world of work.

NYS Leaning Standards:
Career Development and Occupational Studies: Standard 1: Career Development
Career Development and Occupational Studies: Standard 3b: Career Majors
Mathematics, Science, and Technology Standard 5: Technology
English Language Arts Standard 1: Language for Information and Understanding

Resources: Research paper worksheet

Lesson plan/procedure:

Note: This is a good lesson to do with the English teacher.

Assign students a research paper in order to get a realistic picture of a career field. Take the class to the library/career center to complete the worksheet.

As a class review the completed worksheet.

Research should be based on the following resources:
Dictionary of Occupational Titles
Occupational Handbook
Interviews
Files in Library, College, Career Center
Current periodicals and books
Internet

Evaluation: Counselor will evaluate students' understanding of career research through analysis of research paper.

RESEARCH PAPER – RESEARCHING A CAREER FIELD

1. (a) Name the field of work that interests you most. (source and page numbers)

   (b) Are jobs in this field hard or easy to get? Use exact statistics, if available (source and page numbers)

2. What personal characteristics are needed in these fields: independence, neatness, physical strength, creativity, attention to detail, being good with people, leadership, etc. (source and page numbers)

3. List the courses one must take to be qualified in this field. (source and page numbers)

4. Which school catalog(s) did you use? (source and page number)

5. Main duties, you must use the Dictionary of Occupational Titles for job descriptions.

6. School/education requirements (high school, associates degree, bachelor's degree, etc.)

____

____

7. Basic skills required (book keeping, computer programming, driving, typing, etc.)

____

____

8. Working conditions (noisy, late shift, standing, busy/slow times, messy, weekends, etc.)

____

____

____

9. Advancement possibilities

____

____

10. Range of earnings/wages

____

____

11. Additional benefits (travel, vacations, educational reimbursement, etc.)

____

____

____

12. What do you like about the occupation?

____

____

____

____

13. What do you dislike about the occupation?

____

____

____

____

14. What interests and abilities do you have that are related to this work?

____

____

____

15. Have you had any related experience? What is it?

____

____

____

16. What could you do to prepare yourself for this occupation (summer school, part-time work, volunteer work, projects, etc.)?

____

____

____

SECONDARY STAGE:

3 Steps:

1. <u>Becoming Knowledgeable</u> of your career field: acquiring the knowledge or "book learning" necessary for your career preparation: taking classes, getting a degree, attending seminars or workshops, taking training courses, independent reading, TV, etc.

2. <u>Developing Competencies or skills</u> necessary to the work: volunteer work, part-time jobs, apprenticeships, work study, on the job training, etc.

3. <u>Making Career Contacts</u>: People with whom you work and study in the above situations; friends, relatives, teachers, principal, counselors, etc. These people can be most useful by: Giving you information about opportunities, Giving you good recommendations, Giving you introductions to other people who can help you, Providing you with support and encouragement.

MANAGING YOUR FUTURE RESEARCH PAPER

DUE: _______________

1. Use at least 7 sources:
   - want ads
   - Occupational Outlook
   - D.O.T
   - career files
   - interview
   - books / magazines
   - computer / Internet
2. Use outline to answer 1-16. You may number as an outline using title of questions.
3. List sources at the end as a Bibliography.

Lesson 32: What Do You Want To Do?

Name: Bob Germino & Kathy McNally

Grade Level: 9th – 11th

National Standards:
Academic Standard B: Students will complete school with the academic preparation essential to choose from a wide variety of substantial post-secondary options, including college.
Personal/Social Standard A: Students will acquire knowledge, attitudes, and interpersonal skills to help them understand and respect self and others.
Career Standard B: Students will employ strategies to achieve future career goals with success and satisfaction.
Career Standard C: Students will understand the relationship between personal qualities, education, training, and the world of work.

NYS Leaning Standards:
Career Development and Occupational Studies: Standard 1: Career Development
English Language Arts Standard 1: Language for Information and Understanding
English Language Arts Standard 4: Language for Social Interaction

Resources: Black board, chalk or chart paper, and marker

Lesson plan/procedure:

Have students name as many different jobs and careers as possible and list them on the board or chart paper.

Have students answer the following questions:
What do you like to do the most?
What do you like to do for fun?
What things do you do best?
Where do you like to live?
What type of person are you?

Have some students volunteer to share their answers to these questions.

Have the class match their personal qualities of the volunteers with the jobs listed. Have them match up their own personal qualities with the job list. Discuss the education needed for the jobs listed

Evaluation:
Counselor will evaluate students' understanding of matching personalities with jobs through the group discussion.

Lesson 33: Which College is Best for Me?

Name: Kathy McNally

Grade Level: 11th & 12th

National Standards:
Academic Standard B: Students will complete school with the academic preparation essential to choose from a wide variety of substantial post-secondary options, including college.
Personal/Social Standard A: Students will acquire knowledge, attitudes, and interpersonal skills to help them understand and respect self and others.
Career Standard A: Students will acquire the skills to investigate the world of work in relation to knowledge of self and to make informed career decisions.
Career Standard B: Students will employ strategies to achieve future career goals with success and satisfaction.

NYS Learning Standards:
Career Development and Occupational Studies: Standard 3a: Universal Foundation Skills
English Language Arts Standard 1: Language for Information and Understanding
English Language Arts Standard 4: Language for Social Interaction
Mathematics, Science, and Technology Standard 5: Technology

Resources: College choice worksheet

Lesson plan/procedure:

Have students complete the worksheet. You can take them to the Library or Career Center to do the research, and fill out the worksheet.

Use these resources: college guides, catalogues, computer programs, videos.

Discuss with students what they learned about the colleges they researched. What was surprising, disappointing, best/worst thing they found out, did they change their minds about any of the schools or programs after they researched them.

Evaluation:
Counselor will evaluate students' understanding of college information through discussion and information gathered.

WHICH COLLEGE IS BEST FOR ME?

A. Answer the following questions regarding your school of choice.

1. Academic major preference (if any)?
2. Geographic area? Home or away, live on campus or off?
3. School size: small, medium, large?
4. Campus setting: urban, suburban, rural?
5. Student body: coed or single sex, ethnic diversity?
6. Type of school: 2 or 4 year, public or private, religious affiliation?
7. Entrance Difficulty
8. Campus life: activities important to you, fraternities and/or sororities?
9. Special programs: study abroad, co-op, internships, honors program, tutoring, programs for students with disabilities?

B. With the help of your counselor make use of all of the following to research colleges:

College manuals and catalogues
College Fairs
High School and College Career Centers
College Representative Visitors
College Visits
Computer Programs
Videos
Internet

Lesson 34: The College Workshop – Session 1

Name: Louis Bamonte

Grade Level: 11th & 12th

National Standards:
Academic Standard B: Students will complete school with the academic preparation essential to choose from a wide variety of substantial post-secondary options, including college.
Personal/Social Standard A: Students will acquire knowledge, attitudes, and interpersonal skills to help them understand and respect self and others.
Career Standard A: Students will acquire the skills to investigate the world of work in relation to knowledge of self and to make informed career decisions.
Career Standard B: Students will employ strategies to achieve future career goals with success and satisfaction.

NYS Learning Standards:
Career Development and Occupational Studies: Standard 3a: Universal Foundation Skills
English Language Arts Standard 1: Language for Information and Understanding
English Language Arts Standard 4: Language for Social Interaction

Resources: As listed in the outline

Lesson plan/procedure:

Note: These lessons can be used as a guide for students or for counselors.
Follow instructions in the outline.

Evaluation:
Counselor will evaluate students through writing and discussion.

THE COLLEGE WORKSHOP – GUIDE SHEET FOR SESSION 1

1. Introduction to college workshop
   Purpose: to help you learn about yourself and colleges

   A. To help answer questions about college admissions
   B. To help you understand the steps necessary for choosing and applying to colleges
   C. To help you utilize available resources to identify and discover more about colleges that are of interest to you

2. Starting Point - YOU

   A. Career Fantasy – to answer the question: "What do I want to do with my life?"
   B. Discuss: What are my reasons for wanting to go to college? What other choices are there?
   C. Are my goals realistic in terms of my abilities?

3. Preparing for College in Junior Year: Key Ideas:

   A. Stress the importance of planning and organization
   B. Carefully select program of studies
   C. Reflect on what you have to offer
   D. What can you do to make up for lost time

What kind of life would you like? The answer to this question will include choices about:

What kind of job/occupations will you have?
Where will you live?
What kind of people do you want to live and work with?
What values are important to you?
What are your immediate and long term financial needs and desires?
How will you develop your own skills, knowledge, and talents?
What alternative do you want to have available to you?
What role do your family and friends play in your choices?

Lesson 35: The College Workshop – Session 2

Name: Louis Bamonte

Grade Level: 11th & 12th

National Standards:
Academic Standard B: Students will complete school with the academic preparation essential to choose from a wide variety of substantial post-secondary options, including college.
Personal/Social Standard A: Students will acquire knowledge, attitudes, and interpersonal skills to help them understand and respect self and others.
Career Standard A: Students will acquire the skills to investigate the world of work in relation to knowledge of self and to make informed career decisions.
Career Standard B: Students will employ strategies to achieve future career goals with success and satisfaction.

NYS Learning Standards:
Career Development and Occupational Studies: Standard 3a: Universal Foundation Skills
English Language Arts Standard 1: Language for Information and Understanding
English Language Arts Standard 4: Language for Social Interaction

Resources: As listed in the outline

Lesson plan/procedure:

Note: These lessons can be used as a guide for students or for counselors.
Follow instructions in the outline.

Evaluation:
Counselor will evaluate students through writing and discussion.

<u>COLLEGE WORKSHOP</u> GUIDE SHEET FOR SESSION 2

1. Distribute index cards. Have students fill them out as follows
   Name
   1-2 questions about college admissions
   Approximate grade point average

2. Preparing for college in Junior Year
   Carefully select academic program for senior year
   Using the summer to your best advantage:
      Take a course in writing or reading
      Work on advancing an artistic or musical talent
      Working in an area that is related to your career interest
      Travel
      Visit college campuses

3. Steps for planning for college

   A. Take a Self-Inventory: answer these questions:
      What are my goals?
      What are my abilities?
      What are my interests?
      Why do I want a college education?
   Narrow down your choices!

   B. What do I want to study?
   You may already know this, specifically
      computer science
      business administration
      teacher
      marine biologist
   You may already know this, generally
      I want a career in science
      I want a career in humanities
      I want a career in business
   You may not know at all
      This is where "undeclared major" or liberal arts comes in

C. What is my academic level?

   based on program of studies
   based on average
   based on SAT, PSAT, ACT

4. Consider location:
   Where a school is located might be important to you and your family, your budget, and your way of life. What matters to you?

   Does it Matter, yes/no?

   Living in your own state
   Living in a large, urban area
   Living in or near a small town
   Living near scenic beauty
   Living near other schools
   Living in a different climate
   Commuting to school everyday
   Living near your family
   Living on a college campus

5. Consider size:
   Schools vary in size ranging from enrollments of a few hundred to 40,000. There are differences between schools of different sizes. How important are these differences? Do you prefer a large school or a small school?

   Social considerations / Special programs

   co-ed or not
   religious orientation
   athletics
   fraternities, sororities, clubs, organizations
   ROTC
   work-study
   cooperative work programs
   study abroad programs

6. Consider cost:
   Do not rule out a college to early because of cost!

A. Generate a list of possibilities:
    - consult with teachers, parents, and guidance counselor
    - use the GIS
    - use the Index Of Majors

B. Get information on your choices:
    - use the College Handbook
    - use college catalogues
    - speak with college representatives – College Fairs

Lesson 36: The College Workshop – Session 3

Name: Louis Bamonte

Grade Level: 11th & 12th

National Standards:
Academic Standard B: Students will complete school with the academic preparation essential to choose from a wide variety of substantial post-secondary options, including college.
Personal/Social Standard A: Students will acquire knowledge, attitudes, and interpersonal skills to help them understand and respect self and others.
Career Standard A: Students will acquire the skills to investigate the world of work in relation to knowledge of self and to make informed career decisions.
Career Standard B: Students will employ strategies to achieve future career goals with success and satisfaction.

NYS Learning Standards:
Career Development and Occupational Studies: Standard 3a: Universal Foundation Skills
English Language Arts Standard 1: Language for Information and Understanding
English Language Arts Standard 4: Language for Social Interaction

Resources: As listed in the outline

Lesson plan/procedure:

Note: These lessons can be used as a guide for students or for counselors.
Follow instructions in the outline.

Evaluation:
Counselor will evaluate students through writing and discussion.

<u>COLLEGE WORKSHOP</u> GUIDE SHEET FOR SESSION 3

<u>Review of last session:</u>

Steps:

1. Self-Inventory

2. Narrow Choices
   What I want to study
   Academic Level
   Location
   Size
   Social Considerations
   Cost

3. Generate a list of possibilities
   Consult with teachers, parents, and counselors
   Use of GIS
   Use Index of Majors

4. Get information on your choices
   Use College Handbook
   Use College Catalogues/viewbooks
   Speak with college representatives
   Visit campuses

5. Organize your information and evaluate choices
   * Create a chart system in order to compare college choices

	Choice 1	Choice 2	Choice 3	Choice 4
Academics				
Size				
Location				
Social Opp.				
Athletics				
Cost				

6. Discuss your best choices with your School Counselor and Parents
   Select 6-7 colleges to apply to, you may want to you this method
   Minimax Method – 1 long shot school; 3 good shot schools; 2 certain schools

7. Apply:
   Complete applications as soon as possible
   Bring completed applications to counseling office
   Arrange for letters of recommendations
   Arrange for SAT scores to be sent

Lesson 37: The College Workshop – session 4

Name: Louis Bamonte

Grade Level: 11th & 12th

National Standards:
Academic Standard B: Students will complete school with the academic preparation essential to choose from a wide variety of substantial post-secondary options, including college.
Personal/Social Standard A: Students will acquire knowledge, attitudes, and interpersonal skills to help them understand and respect self and others.
Career Standard A: Students will acquire the skills to investigate the world of work in relation to knowledge of self and to make informed career decisions.
Career Standard B: Students will employ strategies to achieve future career goals with success and satisfaction.

NYS Learning Standards:
Career Development and Occupational Studies: Standard 3a: Universal Foundation Skills
English Language Arts Standard 1: Language for Information and Understanding
English Language Arts Standard 4: Language for Social Interaction

Resources: As listed in the outline

Lesson plan/procedure:

Note: These lessons can be used as a guide for students or for counselors.
Follow instructions in the outline.

Evaluation:
Counselor will evaluate students through writing and discussion.

COLLEGE WORKSHOP GUIDE SHEET FOR SESSION 4

Review College Admission Process – from previous sessions.

Time Permitting:
Distribute and review with students the following college preparation materials:

Glossary of Terms for College Bound Students

Warding Off That Rejection Letter – by Richard Haines

SUNY Toward Tomorrow Booklet

Other recent, pertinent material

Allow for Question and Answer Period.

Lesson 38: Career Day

Name: Anne Keary, Heather Bambace and Claudia Rodriguez

Grades: 9-11

National Standards:
Academic Standard A: Students will acquire the attitudes, knowledge and skills contributing to effective learning in school and across the life span.
Career Standard C: Students will understand the relationship between personal qualities, education, training and the world of work.

NYS Standards:
Career Development and Occupational Studies: Standard 2: Integrated Learning
English Language Arts Standard 1: Language for Information and Understanding
English Language Arts Standard 4: Language for Social Interaction

Resources: List of community businesses, faculty and staff.

Lesson plan/procedure:

- Counselors will send out a letter of invitation to the community and school staff for participation
- Select a half day for the event
- Set up classrooms for presenters (AV needs, etc.)
- Through English classes, students will sign up for three workshops on different careers prior to the career day

Evaluation: Students will complete through the English class an evaluation of the day's program. Questions include:

1. Which career workshops did you attend?
2. Did you find the information helpful?
3. Did the your career workshop selection match the results of your self interest inventory?
4. What other career topics would you like your counselor to cover?

Lesson 39: Being Me

Name: Deborah Hardy

Grades: 9-11

National Standards:
Academic Standard A: Students will acquire the attitudes, knowledge, and skills that contribute to effective learning in school and across the life span
Personal/ Social Development: Standard A: Students will acquire knowledge, attitudes and interpersonal skills to help them understand and respect self and others

NYS Standards:
English Language Arts Standard 1: Language for Information and Understanding
Health Standard 2: Maintain a safety environment
Social Studies Standard 5: Civics and character education

Resources: Paper and pencils

Lesson plan/procedure:
- Have students do a cut out of a foot print
- Students write personal qualities and values inside footprint
- Have students share with each other what they wrote
- Bring discussion into larger group setting
- Hang foot prints on a wall for all students to share and be reminded that diversity brings wonderful qualities

Evaluation: Students attending program will experience an understanding of character and respect for diversity.

Lesson 40: Alumni Chat

Name: Deborah Hardy

Grades: 9-11

National Standards:
Academic Standard A: Students will acquire the attitudes, knowledge, and skills that contribute to effective learning in school and across the life span
Personal/ Social Development: Standard A: Students will acquire knowledge, attitudes and interpersonal skills to help them understand and respect self and others
Personal/ Social Development Standard C: Students will understand safety and survival skills

NYS Standards:
English Language Arts Standard 1: Language for Information and Understanding
Health Standard 2: Maintain a safety environment
Social Studies Standard 5: Civics and character education

Resources: Presentation room

Lesson plan/procedure:

- Invite previous graduating seniors for a workshop on college transition
- Meet with current seniors and develop a list of questions for alumni
- Counselor will moderate discussion between both groups. Topics include:
    - Transition to college: friends and roommate
    - Selecting classes
    - What is important to know before you go to college
    - Survival tips for the first year

Evaluation: Students will meet individually with counselor to review discussion and additional concerns.

Lesson 41: Writing for Success

Name: Claudia Rodriguez and Deborah Hardy

Grade: 11

National Standards:
Academic Standard C: Students will understand the relationship of academics to the world of work, and to life at home and community.
Personal/Social Standard A: Students will acquire the attitudes, knowledge, and interpersonal skills to help them understand and respect self and others.

NYS Standards:
English Language Arts Standard 2: Literary Response and Expression
Career Development and Occupational Studies Standard 2: Integrated Learning

Resources: Pen and paper.

Lesson plan/procedure:
1. Meet with seniors in English 12 classes – two sessions for each class.
2. Session I:
    - Students will brainstorm all the activities they have participated in since 9th grade.
    - Students will develop a list of activities and awards and create a resume.
3. Session II:
    - Students will brainstorm topic ideas for college essays based on examples shared.
    - Review paragraph forms and word limits.
4. After each session students share ideas and discuss creativity in the college essay.

Evaluation: Students will develop a resume and draft of a college essay.

Lesson 42: Pressure

Name: Shari Forth

Grade: 9-11

National Standard: *Personal/Social Standard A*: Students will acquire the knowledge, attitudes, and interpersonal skills to help them understand and respect self and others.

NYS Standards:
Career Development and Occupational Studies: Standard 1: Career Development
English Language Arts Standard 1: Language for Information and Understanding
Health, Physical Education, and Family and Consumer Sciences Standards 1: Personal Health and Fitness:
Health, Physical Education, and Family and Consumer Sciences Standards 2: Safe and Healthy Environment

Resources: Chalkboard, chalk, index cards, pen/pencil

Note: This is a two-part activity.

Lesson plan/procedure:

Lead the class in a discussion on pressure. What is it? Where does it come from? How do you know you are experiencing it? How do you deal with it? (Make sure that peer pressure is a major part of this discussion.)

1. Write the words “Physical,” “Social,” and “Emotional” on the chalkboard.
2. Distribute index cards.
3. Have the students write at least on pressure they currently face, or have they recently faced. Emphasize that the cards will be anonymous.
4. Collect the cards.
5. Explain that by using the cards, the pressures that the class has written will be discussed.
6. Read the pressures listed on the cards, then ask the class whether the problem is physical, social, or emotional.

7. How many other students have been in a similar situation? How did they deal with it?
8. Have students interview someone they respect about a time when that person faced a difficult situation.

Evaluation:
At the end of the period, ask the students to summarize what they have learned from the lesson.

Lesson 43: Tolerance and Anti-bias: Role Identity

Name: Ellen S. Bieber

Grades: 9-12

National Standard:
Personal / Social Standard A: Students will acquire the knowledge, attitudes, and interpersonal skills to help them understand and respect self and others.

NYS Learning Standard:
English Language Arts Standard 1: Language for Information and Understanding.

Resources:
Sufficient open classroom Space
"Person Cluster" worksheet for each student
A pen or pencil for each student, extra paper
A flipchart and marker or blackboard and chalk

Lesson Plan / Procedure:

Explain the rationale for this exercise. Hand out the Person Cluster worksheet. Instruct students to put their names in the center and fill out the other 5 circles with 5 groups with which they identify. Encourage participants to choose groups that represent who and what they are. Some examples might be religion, race, ethnic or cultural identification, gender, hobby/activity, family, friend, volunteer activity, language spoken, music or other arts, health / fitness, personality descriptor like caring, optimistic, stressed out, sensitive. Let the students know that there aren't any correct or wrong answers, and that since there are only 5 spaces, that on a different day they might choose 5 different groups to write in.

After students have completed the worksheet, have them break into small groups of 3 or 4 students. Ask 1 person from each small group to create a list of all the identifiers that students

have listed in their molecules. No personal names should appear on the group's list. Collect all lists from the small groups.
Next, ask each student to choose 1 circle that is a primary source of identification. Don't say, "the most," just one that is primary and central. Have the students discuss this in their small group. Why was this their primary identifier? Ask them to discuss the positive and negative aspects of being connected to the one identifier they listed as primary.

As the students continue to discuss, write the small groups' lists on the blackboard or flipchart. Only list each group once.

When the small groups have completed their discussions, conduct a "stand-up." Call out several identifiers from the master list, one at a time, and ask people to stand up, take a quick look around, and then sit down. For example, " Stand up if you would describe yourself as a..." Be sure to call out the items that appeared on a few different lists, as well as others that might not be as common.

Large group discussion: Ask if anyone learned anything about him or herself that was a surprise. Ask how it felt to be the only one standing, or almost alone. Ask how it feels to be part of a large group. Ask students what they can do to ensure everyone in the school can stand with pride and confidence.

Ask each student to flip over the Person Cluster sheet and write an example on the back, of how they can help everyone in the school to stand with pride and confidence.

Collect the worksheets.

Evaluation: Person Cluster worksheet , with written response of how each students can help others in the school to feel confident and proud to be who they are.

PERSON CLUSTER

Directions: 1. Write your name in the body of the person (center)
2. In the other circles (head, hands, and feet) write the names of 5 groups with which you identify.

For sharing: Choose 1 group (a primary identity for you) and answer the following questions:

1. Share a time when you have felt very proud to be a member of that group.

Share a painful experience resulting from membership in that group.

Lesson 44: Fishbowl

Name: Unknown

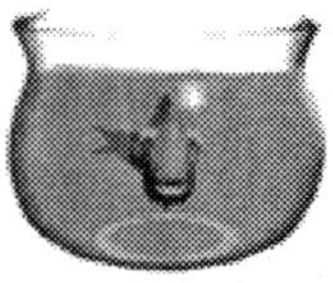

Grades: 9-12

National Standards:
Personal Social Standard A: Students will acquire the knowledge, attitudes, and interpersonal skills to help them understand and respect self and others.

NYS Standards:
Health, Physical Education, and Family and Consumer Sciences
Standard 2: A Safe and Healthy Environment

Resources: Index Cards and pens

Lesson plan/procedure:
Arrange classroom chairs into inner and outward circles. The inner circle chairs should be facing in and not the outside circle. Divide students into two groups: A and B. Group A will sit in the inner circle first. Group B will observe. After five minutes rotate groups.

Establish that the sharing will remain confidential. Each student will write one question they would like to ask their peers on the index card. Moderator has all index cards and shuffles them. A student can select a card and read the question out loud. Each student in the inner circle will have a chance to answer the question. After Group A has finished, have students change seating and Group B will sit in the inner circle. Repeat the process.

Evaluation: Students will write a journal about the experience.

Lesson 45: Reflection

Name: Deborah Hardy

Grades: 9-12

National Standards:
Academic Standard A: Students will acquire the attitudes, knowledge, and skills that contribute to effective learning in school and across the life span.
Personal Social Development Standard A: Students will acquire the knowledge, attitudes, and interpersonal skills to help them understand and respect self and others.

NYS Standards:
Health, Physical Education, and Family and Consumer Sciences: Standard 2: A Safe and Healthy Environment
English Language Arts Standard 1: Language for Information and Understanding

Resources: Pen and paper

Lesson plan/procedure:
Place chairs in a circle. Establish group procedures: confidentiality and passing on topic. Have students write a brief answer to the following topic: " What is the best advice you have ever given someone and why?" When everyone is finished, go around the group and share. Continue discussion on what does it mean to help someone? What resources do teenagers have to help a friend? If you cannot help a peer what should you do? Finish by identifying support staff in the school and the role of the school counselor.

Evaluation: Students will share in writing their understanding of peer support.

Lesson 46: Who's Who

Name: Deborah Hardy

Grades: 9-12 (ESL Students)

National Standards:
Academic Standard A: Students will acquire the attitudes, knowledge, and skills that contribute to effective learning in school and across the life span.
Personal Social Development Standard A: Students will acquire the knowledge, attitudes, and interpersonal skills to help them understand and respect self and others.

NYS Standards:
English Language Arts Standard 1: Language for Information and Understanding
English Language Arts Standard 4: Language for Social Interaction

Resources: List of administrators and staff members

Lesson plan/procedure:

1) Develop a list of job descriptions for administrators, staff members, support staff and any other person a student should know that works in your building
2) Let the staff know that students will be doing a scavenger hunt as an assignment
3) Read the job descriptions and discuss them with the students prior to the scavenger hunt. Students should understand the terminology and what each job is.
4) Students should go find the person whose job description matches and introduce themselves.
5) When all students have matched the names to the jobs, share findings as a group.

NOTE: Some of the matching work can be done in class. Students should find time to meet the staff member and introduce themselves throughout the day.

Evaluation: Students will share their understanding of roles in school.

Lesson 47: Welcome to America/Bienvenidos

Name: Deborah Hardy

Grades: 9-12 (ESL Students)

National Standards:
Academic Standard A: Students will acquire the attitudes, knowledge, and skills that contribute to effective learning in school and across the life span.
Personal Social Development Standard A: Students will acquire the knowledge, attitudes, and interpersonal skills to help them understand and respect self and others.

NYS Standards:
English Language Arts Standard 1: Language for Information and Understanding
English Language Arts Standard 4: Language for Social Interaction
Social Studies Standard 5: Civics, Citizenship, and Government
Health, Physical Education, and Family and Consumer Sciences Standard 2: A Safe and Healthy Environment

Resources: Paper and pen/pencils

Lesson plan/procedure:
1) Discuss with advanced ESL students what their experience has been in the school and what they would have liked to know before arriving to a new country.
2) Have advanced ESL students write about: "What should a new immigrant student, ESL beginner, know about school?"
3) Bring ESL beginners and advanced students together. Pair one advanced to one beginner student. Have the advanced students share their thoughts. If necessary the ESL teacher and counselor can assist in the translation.
4) Ask beginner students to share what they have learned.

Evaluation: Students will share their understanding of acculturation to a new school.

Lesson 48: La Mascara

Name: Deborah Hardy

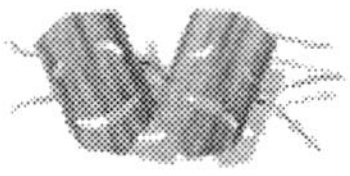

Grades: 9-12 (ESL Students)

National Standards:
Personal Social Development Standard A: Students will acquire the knowledge, attitudes, and interpersonal skills to help them understand and respect self and others.
Personal Social DevelopmentStandard C: Students will understand safety and survival skills.

NYS Standards:
English Language Arts Standard 1: Language for Information and Understanding
The Arts Standard 1: Creating, Performing, and Participating in the Arts
The Arts Standard 2: Knowing and Using Art Materials and Resources

Resources: Coloring pencils, pens or crayons; magazines, glue, scissors and paper masks already cut out.

Lesson plan/procedure:
Give each student a cut out of a mask. Students should color, paste magazine pictures, draw or write on the front of the mask what others see about them, what is visible. Students should turn the mask around and do the same on the back, but what people might not know about them and is unique.

Once the masks are done, have students sit in a circle and share what is on the front of the mask. Go around the circle and have students share one thing that others do not know about them, what is behind the mask.

Evaluation: Students will have a visual representation of their characteristics and qualities.

ASCA National Standards
Index to Lessons
The "Crosswalk"

Academic Development

***Standard A*: Students will acquire the attitudes, knowledge, and skills that contribute to effective learning in school and across the life span.**

Lesson numbers 1, 3, 5, 6, 7, 8, 9, 10, 11, 12, 13, 14, 15, 18, 20, 22, 23, 24, 25, 26, 27, 28, 29, 31, 34, 38, 39, 40, 45, 46, 47

***Standard B:* Students will complete school with the academic preparation essential to choose from a wide range of substantial postsecondary options, including college.**

Lesson numbers 12, 15, 16, 18, 19, 20, 21, 22, 24, 25, 26, 28, 31, 32, 33, 35, 36, 37

***Standard C:* Students will understand the relationship of academics to the world of work, and to life at home and in the community**

Lesson numbers 5, 13, 17, 18, 25, 41

Career Development

***Standard A*: Students will acquire the skills to investigate the world of work in relation to knowledge of self and to make informed career decisions**

Lesson numbers 1, 5, 7, 9, 11, 12, 13, 14, 17, 18, 19, 20, 21, 26, 27, 28, 29, 30, 31, 33, 34, 35, 36, 37

***Standard B:* Students will employ strategies to achieve future career goals with success and satisfaction.**

Lesson numbers 1, 16, 19, 23, 24, 28, 31, 32, 33, 34, 35, 36, 37

***Standard C:* Students will understand the relationship between personal qualities, education, training, and the world of work**

Lesson numbers 1, 3, 6, 8, 9, 10, 12, 13, 14, 17, 23, 26, 27, 28, 31, 32, 38

Personal Social Development

Standard A: **Students will acquire the knowledge, attitudes, and interpersonal skills to help them understand and respect self and others.**

Lesson numbers 1, 3, 4, 5, 6, 7, 8, 9, 10, 11, 12, 13, 14, 17, 20, 21, 23, 25, 26, 28, 30, 32, 33, 35, 36, 37, 39, 41, 42, 43, 44, 45, 46, 48

Standard B: **Students will make decisions, set goals, and take necessary action to achieve goals.**

Lesson numbers 1, 3, 6, 13, 15, 18, 21, 22, 23, 25, 26

Standard C: **Students will understand safety and survival skills.**

Lesson numbers 1, 21, 30, 40, 45, 47, 48

Legend: A:A-1. 1 = Academic Domain, Standard A, Competency I, and Indicator I.
Reprinted with permission from the American School Counselor Association

New York State Learning Standards
Index to Lessons

Health, Physical Education, and Family and Consumer Sciences
Standard 1: Personal Health and Fitness

Lesson number 6

Health, Physical Education, and Family and Consumer Sciences
Standard 2: A Safe and Healthy Environment

Lesson numbers 5, 6, 7, 11, 12, 26, 39, 40, 42, 44, 45, 47

Health, Physical Education, and Family and Consumer Sciences
Standard 3: Resource Management

Lesson number 6

Mathematics, Science, and Technology
Standard 1: Analysis, Inquiry, and Design

Mathematics, Science, and Technology
Standard 2: Information Systems

Mathematics, Science, and Technology
Standard 3: Mathematics

Mathematics, Science, and Technology
Standard 4: Science

Mathematics, Science, and Technology
Standard 5: Technology

Lesson numbers 3, 19, 26, 31, 33

Mathematics, Science, and Technology
Standard 6: Interconnectedness: Common Themes

Lesson number 26

Mathematics, Science, and Technology
Standard 7: Interdisciplinary Problem Solving

English Language Arts
Standard 1: Language for Information and Understanding

Lesson numbers 1, 8, 12, 14, 15, 16, 18, 20, 22, 25, 26, 27, 28, 29, 30, 31, 32, 34, 36, 37, 38, 39, 40, 42, 43, 45, 46, 48

English Language Arts
Standard 2: Language for literary Response and Expression
Lesson number 41

English Language Arts
Standard 3: Language for Critical Analysis and Evaluation:

Lesson numbers 8, 9, 10

English Language Arts
Standard 4: Language for Social Interaction:

Lesson numbers 2, 4, 5, 8, 9, 10, 11, 15, 17, 18, 19, 25, 27, 28, 29, 32, 34, 36, 37, 38, 40, 46

Languages Other Than English
Standard 1: Communication Skills

Languages Other Than English
Standard 2: Cultural Understanding

The Arts
Standard 1: Creating, Performing, and Participating in the Arts

Lesson numbers 2, 48

<u>The Arts</u>
Standard 2: Knowing and Using Art Materials and Resources
Lesson number 48

<u>The Arts</u>
Standard 3: Responding to Analyzing Works of Art

<u>The Arts</u>
Standard 4: Understanding Cultural Contributions of the Arts

<u>Career and Occupational Studies</u>
Standard 1: Career Development

Lesson numbers 1, 2, 5, 11, 14, 15, 16, 17, 18, 19, 27, 28, 30, 31, 32

<u>Career and Occupational Studies</u>
Standard 2: Integrated Learning

Lesson numbers 24, 26, 38, 41

<u>Career and Occupational Studies</u>
Standard 3a: Universal Foundation Skills

Lesson numbers 7, 25, 29, 34, 35, 36, 37

<u>Career and Occupational Studies</u>
Standard 3b: Career Majors

Lesson numbers 16, 17, 19, 24, 28, 29, 31

<u>Social Studies</u>
Standard 1: History of the United States and New York

Lesson number 20

<u>Social Studies</u>
Standard 2: World History

Social Studies
Standard 3: Geography

Social Studies
Standard 4: Economics

Social Studies
Standard 5: Civics, Citizenship, and Government
Lesson 39, 40, 42, 47

Printed in the United States
214536BV00001B/7/A

9 781591 136149